1

Jacobs Well Publishing
45 Buford Lane
Poplarville, Ms 39470
www.jacobswellrecoverycenter.com

Scripture verses referred to in this book are taken
from the most up to date translation of the
New International Version of the Holy Bible
published by Zondervan Publishing House
and provided on line by biblegateway.com

First published by Jacobs Well Publishing
February 2015

ISBN-13:978-0692381366

ISBN-10-0692381368

Printed in the United States of America

Editing Consultant: Julie Keene
Cover design by: Megan Griffin

My Life the Hard Way

{Instead of God's Way}

Dedication

This book is first of all dedicated to my unbelievable and incredible family – specifically my wife Pam and my four children Virginia, Tammy, Susan and Asa – whose loving, forgiving and merciful hearts allowed me to retake a position as loving husband and father that I had foolishly thrown away and in no way deserved to be given back.

This book is further dedicated to the thousands of men and women and the families they represent that have been willing <u>FIRST</u> to share their hopelessness, their desperation, their fear and their failures with me but <u>SECOND</u> and most importantly to share their <u>VICTORIES</u> with me as they walked away from a life of drug addiction to take their rightful place in a new life in Christ.

This book is dedicated to those that have prayed prayers of protection over our ministry over the last fifteen years – knowing that we are rising to our feet <u>every</u> morning to fight the "good fight" against those things of Hell that are focused on destroying our families, our cities, our states and our nation.

But most of all this book is dedicated to my Lord and Savior Christ Jesus who loved me enough to suffer and die on the Cross of Calvary so that in spite of my sick and depraved behaviors in life, I could be forgiven. Without His direct intervention in my life NONE of the other dedications on this page would have been possible.

A little about the author: Pastor Charlie Haynes

I was born in Stamford, Texas in 1944 and shortly after moved to Meridian, Ms where I grew up. I attended Highland Elementary, Kate Griffin Jr. High, and Meridian High School and went on to four years at Livingston State Teachers College in Livingston, AL {now called UWA}. After leaving college I entered the field of retail management with F.W. Woolworth, then Woolco, then TG& Y, then Walmart and finally Marvin's Home Center Stores. That career spanned over 30 years of my life. Early in my career {1966} I married my wife Pamela Smith Haynes from Shucktown, MS{that's right, she was a country girl}. We have four children - Virginia, Tammy, Susan and Asa.

Unfortunately, for me and particularly for my wife and family, I began a downward spiral over those 30 years that led me into behaviours centered totally around the lust of my eyes, the needs of my flesh and the pride of life that turned me into a dark and depraved man, husband and father. In 1996 when my family could take it no longer, my wife asked me for a divorce and my children basically disowned me and then ordered me to get out and don't come back. Only then did I become willing to accept how deep into depravity I had sunk.

And just when I thought all was lost I met a man named Christ Jesus. He has not only saved me, saved my marriage and my family but He has literally transformed me into a totally new creation. What I once thought was the end of everything, I now know was the BEGINNING of everything.

Because I am so grateful for His mercy and loving kindness I have purposed along with my wife and family to spend the rest of my days on this earth sharing the Good News with hopeless and hurting individuals and families that no matter how bad it seems - Christ can redeem it, heal it and restore it. Hence, my wife Pam and I founded Righteous Oaks Recovery Center for Men in Chunky, Ms in 2001 and Jacobs Well Recovery Center for Women in Poplarville, Ms in 2005.

Fun Things I Do: When I'm looking for something to pass the few leisure hours I have these days it's going to generally be spending some quality time with my precious wife Pam or one of my kids or watching one of my 12 grand children or three great grandchildren as they grow. And, there is nothing like pushing out onto the little lake in front of my house and just spending some quality time with God.

Married to: Pamela {Smith} Haynes

Children: I have 4 children, 12 grandchildren and 3 great grandchildren.

Favorite Books (other than the Bible): Obviously, my favorite book is the Holy Bible. But I love surrounding myself with any and all other books that will lead me to a better understanding and daily application of His Word. I'm going to be surrounded by Bible Dictionaries, Concordances, Commentaries and writings of great men and women of God who know how to share, not only the theology of the Word, but the daily application of it.

Favorite TV Shows/Movies: I don't watch much television because honestly there is not much on that is worth looking at anymore but when I do, it will probably be the weather or the history channel.

My Heart's Desire: I live my life today with the assurance of my Salvation, the living proof of my transformation and a burning desire to rise from my bed every morning with only one prayer in my heart. "Lord, until you bring me home to be with you for eternity do not let one day go by that you do not place a broken hurting person in my path that I can give the same hope you have given me in Christ Jesus, Amen."

This Book Is About "Life Lessons" – Lessons I Had To Learn The Hard Way Because I Insisted On Living Life <u>My Way</u> Instead of <u>God's Way</u>.

In my lifelong search for happiness, joy, fulfillment and personal success - my mistakes, my misbehaviors, my missteps, my miscalculations and my misfortunes have littered the pathways of my life.

I have traveled from the Pit of Hell to the Gates of Heaven,

From Desperation to Deliverance,

From Selfishness to Servant Hood,

From the Fear of Failure to Faith in God,

From Hopelessness and Helplessness to the Assurance of God's Saving Grace,

From the Path of Destruction to the Way of Righteousness,

From the Darkness of the Valley of Death to the Glory of that Mountain Top where God resides,

…AND from the Sin of my past to the Promise of my Future in Christ Jesus.

As I have "pressed on toward the goal to win the prize for which God has called me…" I have not looked back, I have not turned back and I have not longed for those things I left behind.

Tonight, I am praying that some of you who are going through some of these things in your life right now can stand on the Victorious Proclamation below.

"I HAVE NOT AND I WILL NOT ALLOW THE SHAME OF MY PAST TO STAND IN THE WAY OF MY FUTURE WITH GOD."

My Life the Hard Way
{Instead of God's Way}
Life Lessons List

1. Many times what looks like the "end of everything" is really just the "beginning of everything."
2. There is a God, and it ain't me, and it ain't you.
3. I am not the "center of the universe."
4. I can't run from my problem, if I'm the problem.
5. If want to be an anchor for others, I've got to get out of "the boat there in."
6. If somebody else is playing "god" in my life – I can bet God is not playing God in my life.
7. The shortest distance between my problems and the solutions to them is the distance from my knees to the floor.
8. What you see is not necessarily what you get.
9. The truth hurts – BUT – knowing the truth will set you free.
10. The biggest lie you will ever tell is the one you tell yourself.
11. The Devil is a trespasser.
12. If I always thank God for the little things, He will always bless me with greater things.
13. The consequences of my life are not left to "chance" but rather to choice.
14. Success in life is not determined by what you have done – rather – it is determined by what you have done ABOUT what you have done.
15. Salvation is a "process".
16. God is not bound by MY circumstances.
17. People do what they do because they believe what they believe.
18. Love is really a "five letter word."
19. The Greatest Gift you will ever give is the "Gift of Forgiveness."
20. If I want to stay free, I've got to stay where I got free at.

Life Lessons I Learned the Hard Way
{from the Word of God}

Life Lesson Number One

1. Many times what looks like "the end of everything" is really just "the beginning of everything."

Proverbs Chapter 14 verse 12 warns us in truth that:

"There is a way that seems right to man but in the end it leads to death."

I have asked myself over and over again, why did it take me so long to believe that truth and why did I insist on learning every life lesson the hard way? If I had only had the good sense much earlier in my life to discover the power and truth of God's Word, I know now, I could have led a much more principled and productive life. But - Oh No! Charlie Haynes, the flesh and blood man, was all about self, all about having it my way, always looking for ways to manipulate the situation or the person I came in contact with - for my benefit. In those days if you wanted to be my friend you could expect to get the "short end of the stick." I was the poster boy for 2 Timothy Chapter 3 Verse 2 which tells us:

"People will be lovers of themselves, lovers of money, boastful, proud, abusive, disobedient to their parents, ungrateful, unholy, without love, unforgiving, slanderous, without self-control, brutal, not lovers of good, treacherous, rash, conceded, lovers of pleasure rather than lovers of God, having a form of godliness but denying

11

its power, the kind who worm their way into the homes of and gain control over weak willed women, who are loaded down with sin and are swayed by all kinds of evil desires, always learning but never able to acknowledge the truth, men of depraved minds who as far as the faith is concerned are rejected.

I am not proud that I fit that description so perfectly up until my early 50s but the truth is that I did.

Ephesians Chapter 1 Verse 11 tells us that:

"In Christ we were also chosen having been predestined according to the plan of him who works out everything in conformity with the purpose of his will."

I have learned the hard way that many times when we demonstrate to God, as I did, that we have no interest in His will or His way or His predestined plan for our life, He will get our attention by giving us a full dose of what we think we want out of life, including a full dose of the consequences that go with it. If I had gotten into the truth of His Word earlier, I could have read the warning for myself when He tells us in Romans Chapter 11 Verse 32 that:

"God has bound all men over to disobedience so that he may have mercy on them all."

But no! I thought I was so slick. I thought I was getting away with all kinds of behaviors that even in my depravity I really knew were not right. Guess what - I wasn't getting away with anything. What I thought I was getting away with, they were talking about at the barber shops and the beauty parlors. I should have believed God's Word in Matthew Chapter 10 Verse 26 through 27 which says:

"So do not be afraid of them. There is nothing concealed that will not be disclosed or hidden that will not be made known. What I tell you in the dark speak in the daylight. What is whispered in your ear proclaim from the rooftops."

Why had I not believed God when He clearly told me in Jeremiah Chapter 17: Verse 10:

"I the Lord search the heart and examine the mind to reward a man according to his conduct - according to what his deeds deserve."

After patiently searching and examining me for over 50 years of my life, God must have determined that the time had finally come when He would be forced to take His hand off of me and turn me over to the disobedience He promised. Without His protective hand on my life {which I never realized was always there} all Hell began to break loose in my life. God literally did a Romans Chapter 1 Verse 18 on me which proclaims:

[18] The wrath of God is being revealed from heaven against all the godlessness and wickedness of men who suppress the truth by their wickedness, [19] since what may be known about God is plain to them, because God has made it plain to them. [20] For since the creation of the world God's invisible qualities—his eternal power and divine nature—

have been clearly seen, being understood from what has been made, so that men are <u>without excuse</u>.

²¹ For although they knew God, they neither glorified him as God nor gave thanks to him, but their thinking became futile and their foolish hearts were darkened. ²² Although they claimed to be wise, they became fools ²³ and exchanged the glory of the immortal God for images made to look like mortal man and birds and animals and reptiles. ²⁴ Therefore God gave them over in the sinful desires of their hearts to sexual impurity for the degrading of their bodies with one another. ²⁵ They exchanged the truth of God for a lie, and worshiped and served created things rather than the Creator—who is forever praised. Amen.

²⁶ Because of this, God gave them over to shameful lusts. Even their women exchanged natural relations for unnatural ones. ²⁷ In the same way the men also abandoned natural relations with women and were inflamed with lust for one another. Men committed indecent acts with other men, and received in themselves the due penalty for their perversion.

²⁸ Furthermore, since they did not think it worthwhile to retain the knowledge of God, he gave them over to a depraved mind, to do what ought not to be done. ²⁹ They have become filled with every kind of wickedness, evil, greed and depravity.

They are full of envy, murder, strife, deceit and malice. They are gossips, ³⁰ slanderers, God-haters, insolent, arrogant and boastful; they invent ways of doing evil; they disobey their parents; ³¹ they are senseless, faithless, *heartless, and ruthless. [32] Although they know God's righteous decree that those who do such things deserve death, they not only continue to do these very things but also <u>approve of those who practice them.</u>*

The final result of that freefall into the Pit of Hell, for me, resulted in a family intervention in my life by my wife, my daughter's, my son, and my son-in-law, who two weeks before Father's Day in 1996 set me down and confronted me with the sin of my life inside and outside of my family. That day my wife rose from the table and called for an immediate end to our 30 year marriage and my children verbally disowned me and declared that I would never hold my grandchildren. As I packed my belongings, got into my old pickup truck, and headed out to nowhere, I thought it was the end of everything. What I did not realize at that moment was that it was actually the <u>beginning</u> of everything. The beginning of a golden opportunity to reach out my hand for the first time ever to a God who has always loved me unconditionally through a Savior that gave his life for me - An opportunity to begin to live by the Spirit and not by the flesh - An opportunity to hold up the darkness of my former life to the brilliant light of God's Word His will and His way for my life - and the opportunity to finally realize that I don't have to continue to learn life's lessons the hard way. This book is the Divine result of that turning point in my life and the lessons I learned the hard way. I hope you enjoy the journey and I pray that you will exercise the wisdom now that it took <u>me</u> so long to exercise.

There are no better principles of living found anywhere other than those that are given to us in God's inerrant and truthful word.

Life Lesson Number Two

2. There is a God, and it ain't me, and it ain't you.

Romans Chapter 1 Verse 20 tells us:

"For since the creation of the world God's invisible qualities his eternal power and divine nature have been clearly seen being understood from what has been made so that man is without excuse."

I knew there was a God; I just didn't want to have any relationship with Him unless I thought it could benefit my flesh in some way. Basically I felt like what little I knew about how He wanted people to live, He would rain on my parade. I'm sure you've seen the Scripture up on somebody's living room wall, over a door or on the doormat out in front of the house that says:

"As for me and my house we are going to serve the Lord."

But have you ever heard the full context of those scriptures which say this:

"But if serving the Lord seems unpleasant to you, then choose for yourself this day whom you will serve.... "But as for me and my house, we will serve the Lord."

Basically, I decided that serving the Lord was <u>not</u> pleasant to me and I decided I would try serving <u>myself</u>. That allowed me to learn another valuable life lesson the hard way. At no point have I ever been or will I ever be in charge of my life. I realize now that if I make the clear choice not to give God charge of my life that inevitably leads to the allowing <u>Satan</u> to take charge of my life. John Chapter 8 Verses 42 through 45 put it this way:

⁴² Jesus said to them, "If God were your Father, you would love me, for I came from God and now am here. I have not come on my own; but he sent me. ⁴³ Why is my language not clear to you?- Because you are unable to hear what I say. ⁴⁴ You belong to <u>your father</u>, the devil, and you want to carry out <u>your father's</u> desire. He was a murderer from the beginning, not holding to the truth, for there is no truth in him. When he lies, he speaks his native language, for he is a liar and the father of lies. ⁴⁵ Yet because I tell the truth, you do not believe me!

As I look back on it now, it was pride that got me. Now I know that God's word says in Proverbs Chapter 16 Verse 18 that:

" Pride goes before destruction and a haughty spirit before the fall."

But back then I reveled in my own genius. I felt like I was the man, there was nothing I could not accomplish if I put my mind to it. Back in those days I began a career in retail management and my mountainous ego thrived in that environment. It was all about climbing the ladder of success, personal ambition and personal recognition often at the expense of others who worked with me. I was going to get to the top of the heap no matter who I had to step on to get there. I wanted to be the "store manager", the one everybody had to look up to, the one everybody had to step and fetch for – you know – god of all that I surveyed. That doesn't fit very well with a God who says in Mark Chapter 9 Verse 35:

"If anyone wants to be first, he must be the very last and the servant of all."

What an awesome lesson it is to learn, that contrary to what we might think, we are not the God of all we survey but rather the creation of the God who is the God of all He surveys. He is God – I am not. He is the creator – I am the created. As God so aptly puts it in Isaiah Chapter 55 Verse 9:

"As the heavens are higher than the earth so are my ways higher than your ways and my thoughts higher than your thoughts."

People like me who cling to self-importance love to jump into intellectual disagreement with others to exercise their self-proclaimed superiority. You and I can lift ourselves up and boost our egos by entering into arguments and debates over life and how we think we should live it which God calls "myths and endless genealogies" in Timothy Chapter 1 Verse four; but, I have learned the hard way that I will never be on an intellectual level with God nor does He need my approval to exercise the plans He has for me:

"plans to prosper me and not to harm me," but rather, "plans to give me a hope and a future" as promised in Jeremiah Chapter 29 Verse 11.

Yes, my friend, I have come to a full understanding that there is a God and it ain't me. And guess what else I learned the hard way; it ain't you either.

Jeremiah Chapter 17 Verse 5 through 8 reminds us:

⁵ This is what the LORD says:

"Cursed is the one who trusts in man,
who depends on flesh for his strength
and whose heart turns away from the LORD.
⁶ He will be like a bush in the wastelands;
he will not see prosperity when it comes.
He will dwell in the parched places of the desert,
in a salt land where no one lives.

⁷ "But blessed is the man who trusts in the LORD,
whose confidence is in him.
⁸ He will be like a tree planted by the water
that sends out its roots by the stream.
It does not fear when heat comes;
its leaves are always green.
It has no worries in a year of drought
and never fails to bear fruit."

And yet, what do you and I do when we run into a personal crisis in our own life or family or friendships? We pick up the phone and call Aunt Sally or Uncle Billy or our next door neighbor or the person alongside us at work to give us the brilliant solution to our own problems when the truth is they can't even solve their own problems. Thank God I have finally come to that place in my life where I have gone from a cursed life by trusting in man to a blessed life by placing complete confidence in God's Word. I had to learn this the hard way, but today I can look you in the eye and confidently state that there is no problem, no dilemma, no situation, no question that will ever arise in your life that God's Word does not warn you in advance about and that His Word does not have the solution for. The more time I have spent in His word seeking His counsel on every issue the more I am convinced that this is true. The next time you face a trial or tribulation in your personal life – I dare you – NO! I <u>double dog</u> dare you – instead of looking for the solution in the advice of Aunt Sally or Uncle Billy, turn to the inerrant truth of God's Word and let Him lead you to the right and righteous solution to the problem.

Life Lesson Number Three

3. I am NOT the "center of the universe."

Mark chapter 9 Verse 35 gives us this account:

"Sitting down Jesus called the 12 disciples and said: If anyone wants to be the first he must be the very last and the servant of all."

Matthew Chapter 23 verse 12 advises us that:

"Those who exalt themselves will be humbled and those who humble themselves will be exalted."

What is it that makes us cling to the infantile notion that the whole world wakes up every morning worrying about what it can do to make us happy and to step and fetch for us all day long?

The Word gives us this wisdom in 1Corinthians Chapter 13 Verse 11:

" When I was a child, I talked like a child, I thought like a child, I reasoned like a child. When I became a man, I put the ways of childhood behind me."

Sadly most people I know including myself cling to the notion that they are the center of the universe long into their adult years. We rise from our beds each morning and are immediately concerned about how <u>our</u> needs are going to get met today and who we can find to meet them – even if it means a sacrifice on their part so that we might benefit. Okay, I know what you're saying – Brother

Charlie, I don't think I am the center of the universe. Oh, yes you do and here is an example for you to consider. You go down to the local Walmart store – you walk in the door expecting to see the door greeter who will acknowledge you and hand you your shopping cart. But there's no greeter! So you wrestle with the carts available and mutter angrily under your breath because they are stuck together and you have to wrestle with them to get one free. Then as you start down the aisle your frustration level jumps as you hear the "tapokita, tapokita,tapokita" of the broken wheel on your cart and so you have to go back for another round of wrestling to get another cart.

You roll up and down the aisles expecting to find someone in a smock or a vest to direct you to the items you are looking for but you can't find anyone anywhere. You finally locate most of the items you want and head toward the checkouts to pay and leave for your next stop which you are already late for. You round the corner to the checkouts {there are 21 of them} where you find that only one is open and there are 25 or 30 people lined up there ahead of you with their buggies brimming over. In frustration you pull up behind the last person in line and begin to openly voice your frustration to the other people in the line. "What the heck is going on here? Why don't they open another check out? Who's managing this place? Can't they see things are backed up?" Why are you so upset? Why are you so frustrated? Why are you blowing off so much steam? I'll tell you why. You think Walmart ought to know that you are in the store and that you are in a hurry and you are now ready to be checked out. Come on – get real now – you're not concerned about anybody else's inconvenience in that line but your own. Your expectations are not being met because this is not what the center of the universe thinker expects.

Here is what the center of the universe thinker expects.

We arrive at the Walmart store and find things are going our way immediately when we find that the nearest parking place to the front of the store is available. As we enter the store we find the door greeter standing at attention and he or she is actually able to greet us by name. "Good morning Mr. Haynes! Thank you for shopping with us at Walmart today." Then the door greeter hands you a shopping cart and says, "Here is a brand-new shopping cart just for you Mr. Haynes. It just came off the truck and the wheels are perfect and well oiled." You smile warmly and start down the aisle with your spectacular new cart and suddenly you hear the click of the PA system being turned on and this is the announcement: "Attention all Walmart Associates! Charlie Haynes has just entered the store. Will all department heads please return to your department in anticipation that Mr. Haynes may need personal service in your area. Make sure that he finds what he needs. And for goodness sake, front end customer service managers, please make sure that all 21 checkouts are open so that when Mr. Haynes is ready to check out he will not have a problem." Come on people! Am I a lying or am I dying? I have had to learn the hard way that people who love God and have a servant's heart never over react to personal inconvenience.

They are not so full of self-importance that they have to be recognized at the door. They don't come unglued because the first cart they get is "whacked." Having to look around a little for what they need gives them more opportunity to fellowship with friends and neighbors they meet in the aisles. And rounding the corner to find only one checkout open and the lines backed up just gives them more time to witness to those who are in line with them. The last time I ran into a backed up lane at the checkouts, I slid up patiently behind the man in front of me. He was a big corn fed boy wearing a camo hat and a Git er Done T-shirt, bermuda shorts and combat boots. He looked back at me and said, "What in the heck is going on here? Why don't they open another check out? Who's managing this place? Can't they see things are backed up? They ought to fire whoever is running this place." At long last I was able to smile warmly to my frustrated new friend and say, "You know what brother, I have learned something the hard way – I am not the center of the universe. This is a busy place and these folks have got a lot of other things going on that require their attention. I'm sure they will get this situation squared away pretty soon." Frustrated by my seeming lack of concern he said: "What are you so happy about?" And I said, "I'm so glad you asked!" and he then got an earful of the Gospel of the Good News of Peace.

Life Lesson Number Four

4. I can't run from my problem when I'm the problem.

My father drank to excess but he forbade my brother and I to drink alcohol until we turned 18. On my 18th birthday he showed up in the living room where I was watching TV and in his hands were two Miller beers. He extended one toward me and said, "Want a beer son?" I took it in my hand and assumed this was like a rite of passage moment for me and my dad. As I lifted the can to my lips to indulge in my first taste of alcohol the aroma of the beer went up my nostrils. It wasn't a pleasant aroma. As I remember it was kind of a pungent odor. I placed the can to my lips and took my first big swallow. Immediately I yanked the can away from my mouth and declared, "Dad this stuff taste awful!" Then, although I didn't realize it at the time, my dad replied with what would become a very prophetic statement when he said: "Don't worry son you'll get used to it." And I did! I not only got used to the taste of beer but vodka, gin and whiskey as well. Then later I got used to amphetamines on top of the alcohol. But because I was able to get up every morning and go to work – surely I wasn't an alcoholic or a drug addict. Or if I was, maybe I was what they call a "functional alcoholic." I worked in retail management with several well-known top retailers and continuously moved up with each of them in spite of my excessive drinking and drug use until it began to consume me. Another lesson I learned the hard way was that you can't run from your problems if you are the problem. Because of my success in retail management my wife and my four children and I moved for promotion 21 times in 18 years. Guess what I discovered? Every time I moved when I got to the next place my alcoholism was waiting there for me. More beer, more alcohol, more pills were waiting there for me. I could not run from my addiction problem because I was the problem. What are you trying to run from? You can't run from a broken marriage, you can't run from stealing from your employer, you can't run from an adulterous relationship, you can't run from perverted behavior, you can't run from addiction to pornography, because where ever you run to it will be waiting for you when you get there. Why – because you are the problem. Not until I was able to confess my problems as sin and repent of them was I able to defeat them.

King David gives us this advice in Psalms Chapter 32 Verses 3- 5:

3 When I kept silent,
my bones wasted away
through my groaning all day long.
4 For day and night
your hand was heavy upon me;
my strength was sapped
as in the heat of summer.
Selah

5 Then I acknowledged my sin to you
and did not cover up my iniquity.
I said, "I will confess
my transgressions to the LORD"—
and you forgave
the guilt of my sin.

Don't run from your problems any longer but rather cling to the advice of Ephesians Chapter 6 Verses 10 - 18 which tell you to:

[10] Finally, be strong in the Lord and in his mighty power. [11] Put on the full armor of God so that you can take your stand against the devil's schemes. [12] For our struggle is not against flesh and blood, but against the rulers, against the authorities, against the powers of this dark world and against the spiritual forces of evil in the heavenly realms. [13] Therefore put on the full armor of God, so that when the day of evil comes, you may be able to stand your ground, and after you have done everything, to stand. [14] Stand firm then, with the belt of truth buckled around your waist, with the breastplate of righteousness in place, [15] and with your feet fitted with the readiness that comes from the gospel of peace. [16] In addition to all this, take up the shield of faith, with which you can extinguish all the flaming arrows of the evil one. [17] Take the helmet of salvation and the sword of the Spirit, which is the word of God. [18] And pray in the Spirit on all occasions with all kinds of prayers and requests. With this in mind, be alert and always keep on praying for all the saints.

I can rejoice in telling you that although I did not lay down in my bed at night sober for almost 20 years of my adult life, I have neither used nor desired to use alcohol or amphetamines or any other mind altering substance for almost twenty years. Standing firm in Christ and no more running from my problems was and is the key to my defeat of those curses.

Life Lesson Number Five

5."If I want to be an anchor for others, I've got to get out of the boat there in."

Have you ever heard the old saying: "Birds of a feather flock together"? Sadly it's true – cuckoos hang out with cuckoos, buzzards hang out with buzzards, turkeys hang out with turkeys, and Eagles hang out with Eagles. One of the things that I have learned the hard way is that Eagles don't ever hang out with turkeys. Turkeys stare longingly into the blue sky and wish they could be Eagles. But, there are not any Eagles soaring above that wish they could fly down and be turkeys. One of the sad truths of life is that as humans we flock to be with people who are in the same misery and misbehavior we are. Somehow climbing in the same boat they are in - in life validates our misery and misbehavior. You know, the old "Everybody's doing that, man" excuse. No, I learned the hard way that it wasn't everybody doing what I was doing – it was just the people I had chosen to flock with – most of them cuckoos, buzzards or turkeys just like me – and all of us in the same boat. I longed to live a better life. I longed to soar with the Eagles. I longed to lead those birds of a feather in my life to something better. And then it dawned on me, if I am ever going to be an anchor of righteousness for others – I am going to have to get out of the boat they are in. In desperation I cried out to God and said, "God, how do I get out of this boat I have found myself in that I might become an anchor for others?" And He said, "Do what Peter did in Matthew Chapter 14 Verses 22 – 32." I rushed to find and reread those Scriptures and there was the answer all along.

Let's look at it together...

²² Immediately Jesus made the disciples get into the boat and go on ahead of him to the other side, while he dismissed the crowd. ²³ After he had dismissed them, he went up on a mountainside by himself to pray. When evening came, he was there alone, ²⁴ but the boat was already a considerable distance[a] from land, buffeted by the waves because the wind was against it.

Do you see it starting already? Christ Jesus soaring up the mountainside {like the Eagle} while the disciples flock together in the same boat.

²⁵ During the fourth watch of the night Jesus went out to them, walking on the lake. ²⁶ When the disciples saw him walking on the lake, they were terrified. "It's a ghost," they said, and cried out in fear.

²⁷ But Jesus immediately said to them: "Take courage! It is I. Don't be afraid."

²⁸ "Lord, if it's you," Peter replied, "tell me to come to you on the water."

²⁹ "Come," he said.

Then Peter got down out of the boat, walked on the water and came toward Jesus.

Then Peter did WHAT?????

Peter got down out of the boat, walked on the water and came toward Jesus!!!

HOW CAN THAT BE?????

Let's examine this a minute. What did Peter do for a living before he met Jesus? That's right, he made his living as a fisherman. All day long, every day, he made his living out on the water, in the boat, fishing. Do you think that there was ever a day when Peter was out in his boat on the sea fishing and realized he had left an important piece of his tackle on shore that he simply turned to someone in the boat with him and said, "Hey Brother, how about you stepping out of the boat, walking on the water back to shore, getting that piece of tackle that we need and walking on water back to the boat so we can use it." – Nope, never happened! Do you think that Peter in all his years on the boat fishing had ever seen <u>anyone</u> walking on the water from the land to a boat or vice versa? Nope, never happened. And yet this man Peter stepped out of the boat he was in and began to walk on water without hesitation.

You can bet your bottom dollar that when Peter started to step out of that boat onto the surface of that tumultuous sea filled with giant waves tossed to and fro by the winds that surrounded those left behind together in the boat, they were yelling at Peter with all their faithless might---"Peter, are you crazy, boy? You better get back in this boat with <u>us</u> before you drown or the sharks get you." But old Peter went anyway and here's why…

Christ Jesus has the power to do <u>two</u> important things. He has the power to <u>Save</u> and He has the power to <u>Transform</u>.

Through the power of Faith, Christ Jesus has single handedly not only gotten Peter out of the boat he was in, but He has also just transformed Peter from a turkey in the boat to an Eagle on the water.

Hebrews 12:1-3 says:

[1] Therefore, since we are surrounded by such a great cloud of witnesses, let us throw off everything that hinders and the sin that so easily entangles, and let us run with perseverance the race marked out for us. [2] Let us fix our eyes on Jesus, the author and perfecter of our faith, who for the joy set before him endured the cross, scorning its shame, and sat down at the right hand of the throne of God. [3] Consider him who endured such opposition from sinful men, so that you will not grow weary and lose heart.

It was a hard lesson that it took me way too many years to learn, understand and apply, that Christ Jesus loves getting cuckoos, buzzards and turkeys out of the boat they're in and transforming them into Eagles. All Peter had to do, all I had to do, and all you have to do is read, believe, receive and apply Hebrews 12:1-3 to your life and the transformation will begin to happen.

The key to continued success is to not allow anything thereafter to get your eyes off Jesus – "the author and perfecter of your faith."

So, now look at verses 30 and 31.

30 But when Peter saw the wind, he was afraid and, beginning to sink, and cried out, "<u>Lord, save me!</u>"

31 Immediately Jesus reached out his hand and caught him. "You of little faith," he said, "why did you doubt?"

Salvation does not guarantee that your life is going to be "Hunky Dory."

As a matter of fact I have learned that too the hard way. I should have read and understood Matthew 16:24

24 Then Jesus said to his disciples, "If anyone would come after me, he must deny himself and take up his cross and follow me."

Walking out your salvation is all about denying self, unselfishness, service and personal sacrifice and doing the right thing in every situation in Christ no matter what comes against you as a result.

Philippians 2:12-13 encourages with this advice:

12 Therefore, my dear friends, as you have always obeyed—not only in my presence, but now much more in my absence—<u>continue to work out your salvation with fear and trembling,</u> 13 for it is God who works in you to will and to act according to his good purpose.

And then this in Matthew 5:11-12:

11 "Blessed are you when people insult you, persecute you and falsely say all kinds of evil against you because of me. 12 Rejoice and be glad, because great is your reward in heaven, for in the same way they persecuted the prophets who were before you.

It is important to recognize that Peter knew Christ. He had been as His side daily as a trusted disciple. He had heard His teaching daily. He had witnessed His miraculous works. And he knew His voice. Once Peter saw Christ on the waters and heard the voice of Christ say – "Come!" – He fixed his eyes on Jesus and his faith carried him forward. But once Peter took his eyes off Jesus and began to become more concerned about the wind and waves surrounding him he began to sink. There is somebody reading the pages of this book right now that has known Christ as your personal Savior – had relationship with Him and have known His voice BUT the storms of life, the uninvited problems, the personal struggles you have faced have taken your eyes off of him and you are sinking. Fear not. I have tidings of great joy. All you have to do is do what Peter did under the same circumstances:

Cry Out!! And He will lift you once again from the muck and mire and place you back on The Rock.

[32] And when <u>they</u> climbed into the boat, the wind died down.

Life Lesson Number Six

6. If somebody else is playing "god" in my life - I can bet that <u>God</u> is not playing God in my life

Exodus 20:4-5 gives us this stern warning inside of the context of The Ten Commandments:

4 "You shall not make for yourself an image in the form of anything in heaven above or on the earth beneath or in the waters below. 5 You shall not bow down to them or worship them; for I, the LORD your God, am a jealous God, punishing the children for the sin of the parents to the third and fourth generation of those who hate me.

When I look back across the generations of my family today I have come face to face with a startling revelation. My grandfather, my father and I were all hard-driving self-motivated men with strong entrepreneurial gifts. By the world's standards we were all considered highly successful admirable men. We were self driven men who got up every morning, put on our fancy suits and ties and marched out into the world to claim success in life. When the real truth was that generationally {deep inside} all three of us were" jacked up" and tore up from the floor up mentally, emotionally, and morally. We were all woman chasers, womanizers, alcoholics and addicts with a depraved and perverted view of life and family and relationships. I don't know that my grandfather, my father or I ever declared openly or publicly that we hated God but there was no fruit born in our lives that demonstrated a love for Him. My gods were always based on those things in life that would satisfy the "lust of my eyes, the needs of my flesh and the pride of life." As I look back on my life there are some things I would do much differently.

*I would have been more careful in choosing my "real" father.

Jesus said in John 8:42:

" if God were your father, you would love me, for I came from God and now am here. I have not come on my own; but he sent me. Why is my language not clear to you?-Because you are unable to hear what I say. You belong to your father, the devil, and you want to carry out your father's desire.

He was a murderer from the beginning, not holding to the truth, for there is no truth in him. When he lies he speaks his native language, for he is a liar and the father of lies. Yet because I tell you the truth, you do not believe me.

{For 52 years of my life, I lived a lie when the truth would have fit better.}

*I would have believed and trusted God instead of men.

This is what the Lord says: "Cursed is the one who trusts in man, who depends on flesh for his strength and whose heart turns away from the Lord. He will be like a Bush in the wastelands; he will not see prosperity when it comes. He will dwell in the parched places of the desert, in a salt land where nobody lives. But blessed is the man who trusts in the Lord, whose confidence is in him. He will be like a tree planted by the water that sends out its roots by the stream. It does not fear when heat comes; its leaves are always green. It has no worries in a year of drought and never fails to bear fruit. {Jeremiah 17:5-8}

{There is no question about life that is not fully addressed in God's Word.}

*I would have done a better job of determining what comes first in my life {God, Family, Work and Play-in that order}

Matthew 6:33 makes us this promise:

" but seek first his kingdom and his righteousness, and all these things will be added.

What things will be added you say? A loving and faithful spouse, loving and respectful children, true and lasting friendships, your needs, the desires of your heart, salvation, redemption, restoration, transformation, not to mention the fruit of the spirit which is love, joy, peace, patience, kindness, goodness, faithfulness, gentleness and self-control. No earthly man ever gave me those things and no earthly man ever will.

*I would have loved others according to God's definition instead of man's.

You can find God's definition of love in 1Corinthians 13:4-8 which says: love is patient, love is kind. Love does not envy, it does not boast, it is not proud. It is not rude, it is not self-seeking, it is not easily angered, it keeps no record of wrongs.

Love does not delight in evil but rejoices with the truth. It always protects, always trusts, always hopes, always perseveres. Love never fails.

I double dog dare you to ask yourself in truth if you are loving yourself, your wife, your children and the significant people in your life by that definition.

*I would have kept my covenant promise {which I did not keep} to my wife made at the altar before God.

"I take you Pamela Sue Smith to be my wedded wife, to have and to hold, from this day forward, for better, for worse, for richer, for poorer, in sickness and in health, to love and to cherish, till death do us part, and thereto forsaking all others I pledge you my faith and love."

*And loved her always as His Word instructed in:

Ephesians 5:25-29:

"Husbands, love your wives, just as Christ loved the church and gave himself up for her to make her holy, cleansing her by the washing with water through the word and to present her as a radiant church, without stain or wrinkle or any other blemish, but holy and blameless. In this same way, husbands ought to love their wives as they love their own bodies. He who loves his wife loves himself. After all, no one ever hated his own body, but he feeds and cares for it just as Christ does the church.

*I would have loved my children and protected them rather than use them.

Matthew 18:2-6:

"He called a little child and had him stand among them. And he said:" I tell you the truth, unless you change and become like little children, you will never enter the kingdom of heaven. And whoever welcomes a little child like this in my name welcomes me. But if anyone causes one of these little ones who believe in me to sin, it would be better for him to have a large millstone hung around his neck and be drowned in the depth of the sea."

*I would have applied God's greatest commandments to all my relationships with, employees, friends, acquaintances and family.

Matthew 22:36-39:

"Teacher, which is the greatest commandment in the law? Jesus replied: love the Lord your God with all your heart and with all your soul and with all your mind. This is the first and greatest commandment. And the second is like it: love your neighbor as you love yourself."

"*I would have "believed" God, and not just "believed in" God.

James2:23:

"And the Scripture was fulfilled that says, Abraham believed God, and it was credited to him as righteousness, and he was called God's friend."

James tells us further in Chapter 2 Verse 19 that even the demons in hell believe in God and shudder. You will find

DRAMATIC improvement in your walk with God when you go from just believing in God to believing God.

*I would have received and believed that I was in a daily battle for my very soul and put on and kept on the wisdom and the armor of God.

Ephesians 6:10-12:

"Finally, be strong in the Lord and in his mighty power. Put on the full armor of God so that you can take your stand against the devil's schemes. For our struggle is not against flesh and blood, but against the rulers, against the authorities, against the powers of this dark world and against the spiritual forces of evil in the heavenly realms."

*And finally, I would have met no one that I did not subject to the final command given to me by my Lord and Savior Jesus Christ.

Matthew 28:18:

"Then Jesus came to them and said, all authority in heaven and on earth has been given to me. Therefore go and make disciples of all the nations, baptizing them in

the name of the father and of the son and of the Holy Spirit, and teaching them to obey everything I have commanded you."

Revelation Chapter 12 Verse 11 boldly states that *"we have overcome the devil by the blood of the lamb and the word of our testimony."* The Lamb of God has already shed his blood at the Cross of Calvary. I will spend the rest of my life giving my living testimony of what He has done for me to those who are broken and hurting and HOPELESS.

Those generational curses that I talked about at the beginning of this chapter were broken off my life and my family that night I dropped to my knees in the den of my home and cried out to God for forgiveness, Salvation, transformation and redemption. If you are reading this book and you have found your life, your marriage, your family or your relationships on the rocks of destruction, I strongly recommend that you drop to your knees and immediately follow the advice given by our Father in Heaven in 2Chronicles 7:14 which says:

" if my people, who are called by my name, will humble themselves and pray and seek my face and turn from their wicked ways, then I will hear from heaven and will forgive their sin and will heal their land. Now my eyes will be open and my ears attentive to the prayers offered in this place."

Life Lesson Number Seven

7. The shortest distance between my problems and the solutions to them is the distance from my knees to the floor.

Most experts agree that the first and most significant sign that there is a breakdown in a love relationship is when people stop talking to each other. Come on and go back down memory lane with me. I mean go on back to your teenage years and your "first love." Remember how you longed 24/7 to be alone with them or just to hear their voice? I remember picking up my first love for a date as early as six o'clock in the afternoon. Because I loved and respected her I would open the passenger door of my car for her, but once I got in on my side I would of course expect her to slide across the seat and sit close to me. Generally, I would hold the steering wheel with only my left hand because my right arm would be wrapped around her shoulders. We would talk all the way to the movie theater where once seated inside I would reassert my position of closeness by putting my arm around her in the movie. Yes I would watch the movie but I was much more interested in being with her and talking to her and holding her than what was going on on the movie screen. After the movie I still wanted to be with her so I would take her out for a bite to eat where we would spend more time talking. I enjoyed the food but not as much as being with her and talking to her. Then much to my regret I would have to get her home before her curfew. Of course there would be hugs and kisses and then me getting in my car and driving home as quickly as possible so that I could do – <u>what</u>? That's right! Get on the phone and call her up so I could talk to her even more. There were many nights that we literally went to sleep while talking on the phone – woke up the next morning and there's the phone laying on the floor beside the bed still off the hook. Oh Yeah!! I'm so sure I'm the only one who's ever done that. When you really love someone you want to spend every waking moment you can with them in person or in conversation. I want to suggest to you that our relationship with God through Christ Jesus should be no different. Our unwillingness to set aside intimate personal time talking with Him, fellowshipping with Him and adoring Him is a sure sign that there is a breakdown in the relationship.

Prayer is nothing more than private, personal, loving conversation with God.

So, if we <u>do</u> consider God our first love, why does it seem so difficult to build and practice a strong and meaningful prayer life? I believe it is because we don't know how to pray or what to pray. Don't be discouraged. We are in good company. Even Christ's disciples did not know how to pray. And it bothered them enough that they went and asked Him to teach them how to pray.

Luke 11:1- "One day Jesus was praying in a certain place. When he finished, one of his disciples said to him, Lord, teach us to pray just as John taught his disciples."

The answer he gave is available to each of us in the New Testament writings. So let's look how Jesus answered the disciples in Matthew 6:9 and following…

*"This then, is **<u>how</u>** you should pray:"*

It is important that we recognize that Jesus was telling us this is **how** you should pray not **what** you should pray. Yet we have turned this prayer lesson into a recitation that we call the Lord's Prayer. I don't believe Christ ever intended it to be a recitation but rather a line by line explanation of **how** to have a meaningful conversation with our Father in Heaven. So let's just look at it verse by verse and try to understand the lesson being taught.

"Our father in heaven,"

Why did he start with that opening and what is the significance of it? I believe Christ was instructing us about the importance of understanding the positional difference between man and God when approaching Him in prayer. Simply put He is God and we are not. We are approaching the God who loved us so much that He allowed His only Son to suffer and die on the Cross of Calvary for our sins and for our sake so that through our faith in Him we might not perish but rather have everlasting life. You approach someone that important to you in brokenness, humility, reverence and respect.

We need to understand that when we approach Him to open the conversation.

"Hallowed be your name,"

To "hallow" someone or something means to "set apart as Sacred or Holy." As I enter the presence of God in humbleness, I want Him to know that I know who He is and how deeply grateful I am to Him for all He has done in my life. On my knees I openly declare that He is Yahweh; He is Jehovah, the I Am, the Alpha and Omega, the God of

44

Abraham, Isaac and Jacob, the Creator of all things in Heaven and Earth, the God and Father of my Lord and Savior Jesus Christ. He is the breath I am breathing. He is every beat of my heart. He is the soundness of my mind. He is the health of my body and the soundness of my frame. And He is my full portion. I want Him to hear me say something like that every time I begin my conversation with Him in Prayer.

"Your Kingdom come,"

Practicing Christians – those that walk out their daily lives constantly and consistently by applying the sound biblical principles in God's Word to their life, fully understand, that for a season they are in this world but they are not a part of this world.{In other words we are just passing through this world on the way to our eternal home in the Kingdom of Heaven}. I feel it is very important that we openly acknowledge, confirm and confess in our prayers that it is the desire of our heart to be Kingdom citizens rather than worldly citizens. We should ask God in prayer to strengthen us against the danger of beginning to define our life's worth and success by what men think and rather define our life only by what God thinks about our service to Him and our fellow man.

"Your will be done on Earth as it is in Heaven."

This verse is extremely important because it embodies our deep desire to let God know in prayer that we want to live every day of our life according to His will not ours-by His plan not ours-by His laws and commands, not ours. There are many of you reading this book who have been trying to

45

do it your way most of your life and all it has brought is heartache and hopelessness.

I want to remind you that Proverbs 14:12 warns us that:

"There is a way that seems right to man, but in the end it leads to death."

I know full well what it is to live most of your adult life on the "my way or the highway thinking." It almost destroyed my marriage, my family, my friendships and my future and had I not met a man named Christ Jesus and adopted this attitude reflected in Psalms 119:33-40 I would have lost them:

"Teach me, old Lord, to follow your decrees; then I will keep them to the end. Give me understanding, and I will keep your law and obey it with all my heart. Direct me in the path of your commands for there I find delight. Turn my heart towards your statutes and not toward selfish gain. Turn my eyes away from worthless things; preserve my life according to your word. Fulfill your promise to your servant, so that you may be feared. Take away the disgrace I dread, for your laws are good. How I long for your precepts! Preserve my life in your righteousness.

" Give us this day our daily bread."

Christ is indicating to us in this verse that <u>after</u> we have spent time understanding the positional difference between ourselves and our Father in Heaven; <u>after</u> we have understood the importance of beginning the conversation by "hallowing" His name; <u>after</u> we have confessed our desire to be guided by His Kingdom principles and not the world's and after we have confessed our failures as a result of living by our will and cried out to want only His will for our life; there comes a time in the conversation with God to lift up our needs, our petitions and our grievances. Unfortunately, you and I usually jump into our conversations with God with only what we need, what we feel and what we are worked up about. Always position yourself Spiritually with God before you launch into telling Him why you REALLY stopped by to talk to Him. Do you get what I'm saying???

"Forgive us our debts,"

The acknowledgements of our sins before God in prayer are powerful and important. You may have heard the old saying: "I'm not as good as I need to be but I'm a lot better than I used to be." Learning to live your life for Christ is a lifelong process. You don't just receive Christ as your Savior and find yourself living a completely righteous life.

Be reminded of the fact that Philippians 2:12-13 says:

" Therefore, my dear friends, as you have always obeyed – not only in my presence, but now much more in my absence – continue to work out your salvation with fear and trembling, for it is God who works in you to will and to act according to his good purpose.

When I hit my knees that night at the end of my rope I found hope in the confession of my sins before God. I found myself in a 2Corinthians 7:9-11 moment when God said:

" ...yet now I am happy, not because you were made sorry, but because your sorrow lead you to repentance. For you became sorrowful as God intended and so were not harmed in any way by us. Godly sorrow brings repentance that leads to salvation and leaves no regret, but worldly sorrow brings death. See what this godly sorrow has produced in you: what earnestness, what eagerness to clear yourselves, what indignation, what alarm, what longing, what concern, what readiness to see justice done.

Neither you nor I will ever reach perfection on this earth. Perfection comes when we see our Savior face to face. But our lives will grow more righteous day after day as we strengthen our walk in Christ day by day. Prayer allows you to keep your sins and your short comings before God "under the blood." Your sins and shortfalls will always be with you in this life but they will be different. You see I don't have to worry today about confessing the sin of alcohol abuse, drug abuse, infidelity to my wife, neglect and abuse of my children, lying, stealing and manipulation and many of the other depraved behaviors I once lived because I have been completely delivered from those things through my belief and life in Christ. I still fall short today – even as a Pastor. But my sins and short comings now are centered on how well I am walking out my faith in God as a living testimony of what He can do for a seemingly lost and hopeless man and how dedicated I remain on a daily basis in helping others find the same hope I have found in Him.

"as we have also forgiven our debtors."

Every time I look at this verse and think of the power of what it means, I have to stop and say to myself, "Hold on now! Do I really want God to forgive me of my sins today exactly the same way that I have been forgiving other people that have sinned against me?" You and I are always wanting to receive forgiveness for the things we know we have done wrong but we are very seldom as quick to forgive those who have used, abused or misused us. Be careful. God's got a pretty strong stand on that – Matthew 6:14-15

> *" For if you forgive men when they sin against you, your heavenly father will also forgive you. But if you do not forgive men their sins, your father will not forgive your sins ".*

And again in Matthew 7:1-2:

> *" Do not judge, or you too will be judged. For in the same way you judge others, you will be judged, and with the measure you use, it will be measured to you. "*

Christ Jesus placed this important point on how to pray in His example to the disciples because He wanted us to understand that forgiveness is a **BIG DEAL** to our Father in Heaven. After all, He sent His Son to this Earth to suffer and die on the Cross of Calvary so that we might – what? That's right – be forgiven.

Our Saviors Dying Request - Luke 23:33-34:

> *" When they came to the place called the skull, there they crucified him, along with the criminals – one on his right,*

*the other on his left. Jesus said, father, forgive them, for
they know not what they do.*

I have learned that there are four kinds of forgiveness: the
forgiveness of God, forgiving myself, forgiving others, and
others asking for my forgiveness. You and I control three
of those types of forgiveness and one we do not. It is very
important to understand the difference. YOU control the
forgiveness of God because He has promised that the
moment you receive His Son – Christ Jesus as your Savior
– your sins will be forgiven. YOU have the power to
forgive yourself for the mistakes you have made in life
through your faith in God. For you not to forgive yourself
is an abomination in the eyes of God.

Not forgiving yourself is like saying to God that His Son's
death on the Cross and His Blood shed there was just not
sufficient in your opinion to cover YOUR sins. We have
already discussed previously how God feels about your
unwillingness to forgive others who have sinned against
you. The one type of forgiveness you DO NOT control is
others asking you for forgiveness for the things they have
done to hurt you. You may or may not ever receive that
forgiveness. But what I have discovered by experience
about that type of forgiveness is that in time God will
always work it out where He thinks the relationship is
important enough that it needs to be reconciled. Just trust
Him on that one.

"And lead us not into temptation,"

I have learned the hard way that it is a foolish man who
thinks that he is so strong willed that he cannot be tempted
to fall into the temptation to do something that is beneath

him. Since the fall of Adam, man has been born into a sin nature. It is only when we gain the heart and mind of Christ that we can begin to defeat those moments of weakness that can overcome us and lead us down the wrong path in life. God discusses this weakness with us often throughout His Word.

In James 1:12-15 there is this:

" Blessed is the man who perseveres under trial, because when has stood the test, he will receive the crown of life that God has promised to those who love him. <u>When tempted</u>, no one should say, God is tempting me. For God cannot be tempted by evil nor does he tempt anyone; but <u>each one is tempted when, by his own evil</u> desire, he is dragged away and enticed. Then after desire has conceived, it gives birth to sin: and sin, when it is full grown, gives birth to death."

Notice, God does not say in the Scriptures above: "<u>IF</u> you are tempted, he says <u>WHEN</u> you are tempted." My experience has been that God will not tempt you BUT He will allow you to be tempted and tested often because He knows that the practice of taking victory over those tests, trials and temptations will build perseverance and character in you day by day. You will never live long enough nor perfect your walk with Christ well enough that you will not be tempted and tried-Satan will make sure of that.

That is why Christ has advised us to keep always as a part of our daily prayer the confession to ourselves and to God that we are human and therefore subject to fail by succumbing to the lust of our eyes, the needs of our flesh and the pride that is in us. I found a lot of comfort in 1Corinthians 10:13 which says:

" No temptation has seized you except what is common to man. And God is faithful; he will not let you be tempted beyond what you can bear. But when you are tempted, he will also provide a way out so that you can stand up under it. "

You and I <u>have been</u> and <u>will continue to be</u> tempted to fall into the exact same ungodly behaviors. We all have been or will be tempted to lie and cheat and manipulate and steal and covet and rob and seek revenge and many other things in life. What separates us and determines the quality of our character is whether or not we succumb to those temptations. The scripture above boldly states that God will not let you be tempted beyond what you can bear so maybe your asking yourself the same question I once asked God in a moment of frustration and failure – God why couldn't I bear this temptation? His answer – <u>YOU DIDN'T WANT TO BEAR IT!!!</u>

Only one flesh and blood man ever has and ever will walk this earth that did not succumb to temptation. His Name was Jesus Christ. This is what Hebrews 4:15 says about Him:

" For we do not have a high priest who is unable to sympathize with our weaknesses, but we have one who has been tempted in <u>every way</u> just as we are – yet was without sin. "

Before entering the ministry, I spent 35 years in retail management with Woolworth, Woolco, TG&Y, Walmart and finally a great mom-and-pop hardware and building materials company called Marvin's Home Center Stores. My first management position with Marvin's was in a brand-new 50,000 square-foot store being opened in Meridian, Mississippi. The store boasted a full line hardware store, building materials store, lumberyard and a beautiful lawn and garden center. I remember just prior to grand opening being instructed to hang up a huge banner on the front fence of the lawn and garden area that said: "Live Plant Guarantee! If you buy a plant, shrub or tree from Marvin's and it dies within 12 months of your purchase, we will replace the plant or give you a refund."

I looked at the sign and thought about how many flowers, shrubs and hanging baskets I had killed in my lifetime due to improper care and watering. I remember thinking to myself that someone in the corporate office must have lost their mind. But not wanting to question the policy, I hung the banner as instructed with a wait and see attitude. That spring and summer came and went without a problem. The new store was a great success and the lawn and garden area was booming with business. But the next year as the spring planting season started I was summoned from my office by the customer service desk saying, "There is a lady down here insisting on talking to the store manager." As I approached the customer service desk I observed a little old lady standing there, looking around and patting her foot while holding three or four small, scraggly, dead looking trees in her hand. I smiled warmly and said, "May I help you ma'am?" And she replied rather abruptly and firmly, "Are you the store manager?" "Yes ma'am I am." And then she started in: "That sign you all have posted outside that says you guarantee your plants for a year – is that right?" " Yes ma'am it sure is," I replied confidently. "Well, I bought these Bradford Pear trees in here last summer and planted them just like the instructions said and they ain't had narry pear on 'em yet." I hesitated for a moment trying to figure out how {without ticking this lady off more than she already was} how I was going to explain to her something she obviously did not know or even worse did not want to hear. I began cautiously, "Well ma'am, you probably didn't know this but the Bradford Pear is an 'ornamental' fruit tree and it flowers but it does not have pears on it. You know, like a Flowering Cherry or a Flowering Peach or a Flowering Crab Apple. They have beautiful flowers on them but they don't bear fruit." What that little old lady said in response to that piece of unexpected information has remained in my heart and my mind from that day forward. She pulled her shoulders back, stuck her bony little finger in my face and said: "Let me tell you something young man. If something is going to leaf out, be covered with blossoms and call itself a Bradford Pear tree, I think I ought to have a reasonable expectation that it's going to have pears on it!!!" And there it was…

Life Lesson Number Eight

8. What you see is {not necessarily} what you get.

Matthew 7:15-20 clearly warns us:

> *"They come to you in sheep's clothing, but inwardly they are ferocious wolves. By their fruit you will recognize them. Do people pick grapes from thorn bushes, or the figs from thistles? Likewise, every good tree bears good fruit, but a bad tree bears bad fruit. A good tree cannot bear bad fruit, and a bad tree cannot bear good fruit. A tree that does not bear good fruit is cut down and thrown into the fire. Thus, by their fruit you will know them."*

Why are you and I constantly being tricked by the outward appearance of persons, places and things? I have come to the place in my life where I firmly believe that the answer to that question is as old as the weaknesses found in man in the Garden of Eden. The problem is seated in our willingness to listen to and accept the lies we are told {or even worse that we tell ourselves}, a willingness that is based on the lust of our eyes, the needs of our flesh and the pride of life. My daughter has a life lesson of her own that she shares often:

"When somebody shows you who they are – BELIEVE THEM!!!

In my old life, I could clean up, comb my hair, brush my teeth, slap on a little deodorant and cologne, suit up in a shirt and tie, put on some spit shined shoes, a big smile, a wink and a line of bull and get just about anything I wanted out of life. But, unfortunately, <u>you</u> would be getting the short end of the stick in the friendship or relationship because what you saw in me {on the outside} was as far and away from who I was on the inside as you could imagine. I was a walking living example of the kind of person that Christ was talking about in Matthew 28:25 – 28 when He said:

" Woe to you... You hypocrites! You clean the outside of the cup and dish, but inside you are full of greed and self-indulgence. First clean the inside of the cup and dish and then the outside will also be clean. Woe to you... you hypocrites! You are like whitewashed tombs, which look beautiful on the outside but on the inside are full of the bones of the dead and everything unclean. In the same way, on the outside you appear to people as righteous but on the inside you are full of hypocrisy and wickedness.

That was the old me. Putting forth the false outward impression that I was one of the good guys when in reality on the inside I was so dark, so depraved and so devious that comparatively speaking I made Freddy Kruger look like Tom Cruise. The only way I could continue day after day to live that life was to continue to lie to myself day after day about who I REALLY was on the inside. "It's what's on the inside that counts" is not only a powerful truth but it is also a biblical truth. Life has taught me the hard way that our lies will always be exposed and the truth uncovered. What I thought I was getting away with they were talking about around the water cooler. Why are we so self deceived that we cannot grasp the biblical truth that I talked about earlier put forth in Luke 12:3 which tells us:

"What you have said in the dark will be heard in the daylight, and what you have whispered in the ear in the inner rooms will be proclaimed from the rooftops."

Romans 11:32 tells us that:

"God has turned all men {and women} over to disobedience so that He can have mercy on them."

It wasn't until God did that for me that I was able to ask myself a life changing question. The question was – "Charlie Haynes, truthfully, who are you trying to make people think you are and who are you – REALLY?" Have you ever truthfully examined yourself and asked yourself that question? My experience has taught me that we need to, because sooner or later – one way or another – the truth is going to surface in our life concerning "who we really are" and the results of that revelation {if we are not the same person inside and out} are going to be heart breaking, not only for us, but for the people in our lives that "THOUGHT" they knew who we were.

Luke 6:45 cautions us:

"A good man brings good things out of the good stored up in his heart, and an evil man brings evil things out of the evil stored up in his heart. For out of the overflow of the heart the mouth speaks."

In other words, no matter how hard we try to disguise them or hide them - when jostled, or pushed, or challenged, or angered, our true faults, or weaknesses, or prejudices, or hatred, or depravity will be exposed to the light of the truth. I want to close this chapter by urging you to not only have the courage to examine whether or not <u>you</u> are the same person morally inside and out but teach yourself to be diligent about whether or not the people you associate with in life are the same inside and out morally. Do not let the deciding factor in who you spend the rest of your life with or who you call your best friend or confidant be their outward appearance or outward behavior. Go deeper than that in your assessment of their true character. Pray and ask God to give you an extra measure of wisdom and discernment concerning your important relationships. In 1981, a blind country music artist named Terri Gibbs recorded a chart topping song whose words have rung in the hearts of men and women since the beginning of creation and still haunt us even until this day. Listen to the penetrating words of this song called:

Somebody's Knockin'

Somebody's knocking
Should I let him in the
Lord it's the devil
Would you look at him
I've heard about him
But I never dreamed
He'd have blue eyes and blue jeans

Well somebody's talkin'
He's whispering to me
Your place or my place
Well which will it be
I'm getting' weaker
And he's comin' on strong
But I don't wanna go wrong

Come on people! Lay aside the "lust of the eyes, the needs of the flesh, and the pride of life" and approach every relationship with the same approach that God tells us He uses when choosing "a man after His own heart."

1Samuel 16:7:

But the Lord said to Samuel," Do not consider his appearance or his height, for I have rejected him. The Lord does not look at the things people look at. People look at the outward appearance, but the Lord looks at the heart."

Life Lesson Number Nine

9. The truth hurts! – BUT – "Knowing the truth will set you free."

We looked at this scripture briefly back a little while ago but I know of no better place to start concerning this powerful life lesson than in Ephesians 6:10-18. So let's just look at it together again for a minute.

"Finally, be strong in the Lord and in his mighty power. Put on the full armor of God so that you can take your stand against the devil's schemes. For our struggle is not against flesh and blood, but against the rulers, against the authorities, against the powers of this dark world and against the spiritual forces of evil in the heavenly realms. Therefore put on the full armor of God, so that when the day of evil comes, you may be able to stand your ground, and after you have done everything to stand – stand firm then, with the belt of truth buckled around your waist, with the breastplate of righteousness in place, and with your feet fitted with the readiness that comes from the gospel of peace. In addition to all this, take up the shield of faith, with which you can extinguish all the flaming arrows of the evil one. Take the helmet of salvation and the sword of the Spirit, which is the word of God. And pray in the spirit on all occasions with all kinds of prayers and requests. With this in mind, be alert and always keep on praying for the Saints."

In these Scriptures, our Father in Heaven offers us seven powerful weapons that will allow us to defeat the rulers, the authorities, the powers of darkness, and the spiritual forces of evil that will certainly come against us daily. I submit to you that I firmly believe that we cannot begin to effectively put on and use the breastplate of righteousness, the feet fitted with readiness, the shield of faith, the helmet of salvation, the sword of the Spirit or prayer until we have Weapon Number One {The Belt of Truth} firmly in place in our life. Let's be reminded for a minute what Christ Jesus has to say about this powerful, life-changing, indispensable thing called TRUTH. In John 8:44-45 Christ warns those of us living for the world that:

"We belong to our father, the devil, and we want to carry out his desires. That he {the devil} was a murderer from the beginning, not holding to the truth, for there is no truth in him. When he {the devil} lies, he speaks his native language, for he is a liar and the father of lies. {But then Christ says} Yet because I tell you the truth, you do not believe me."

In John 14:6 Jesus said:

"I am the way and the truth and the life. And no one comes to the Father except through me."

To put it another way because Jesus is truth and we can only come to God through Him, we must therefore come to God in truth. In John 4:23 Christ said to the woman at the well:

"Yet a time is coming and has now come when the true worshipers will worship the Father in Spirit and in Truth that they are the kind of worshipers the Father seeks.

Psalm 15:1-2 gives us this penetrating question and answer:

" Lord who may dwell in your sanctuary? Who may live on your holy hill? The answer – he whose walk is blameless and who does what is righteous, who speaks the truth of his heart.

And then in Psalms 86:11 there is this lament:

" Teach me your way, Oh Lord, and I will walk in your truth; give me an undivided heart, that I may fear your name."

Before we can effectively put on the "Belt of Truth" we must be willing to first take off the "Belt of Lies" that the devil has given us. In order to ensure that we have the ability to lie our way out of almost any situation the devil gives us at least three belts: 1.the Belt of Half-Truths {aka the "what they don't know won't hurt 'em belt"} 2.the Belt of Wicked Devices{aka the embellishment, gossip, slander and dissensions belt} 3.the Belt of Manipulation{aka the belt able to stretch and bend the truth to fit any evil circumstance}.

NOTE: WE ONLY NEED ONE BELT OF TRUTH BECAUSE NO MATTER WHO WE ARE, IT FITS JUST RIGHT!!!

Now let's talk for a minute about this thing called the "Belt of Truth"- how to put it on and how to use it.

In order to put on and effectively use the Belt of Truth in our life we must finally begin to take personal responsibility for who we are, what we have become, what we have done and be willing to face the consequences we have created by our own actions- without blaming others.

62

You are going to have to look into what I call the spiritual mirror of life and take a long hard look at what you see in that mirror. Don't just look into the mirror like you normally do when you fix your hair, put on your makeup, trim your beard or whatever other beautifying ritual you use the mirror for daily but rather look deep into your own soul – muster a courage to begin doing something you may have never done before – examine your heart instead of your outward appearance and behavior. A good friend once shared this little poem with me and I have held on to it and treasured it as sound wisdom:

I have six honest serving men,

I'll keep them till I die.

Their names are Who and What and Where

And When and How and Why

Ask yourself:

Who do you try to make others "think you are" and in reality "Who are you?"

What do you think "God created you to "do with your life" and "What have you done about it?"

Where did you "hope you would find yourself at your age" and "Where are you now?"

When was the last time you told yourself – "I cannot live this way anymore" and "When are you really going to do something about it?"

How did you "get yourself into this mess" and "How are you going to get yourself out of it?"

Why have you "never considered Christ Jesus as the answer" and "Why don't you consider Him now?"

There is an awesome life changing promise awaiting you in the "spirit mirror" of life! That promise was made in John 8:32:

" Then you will know the truth, and the truth will set you free."

Life Lesson Number Ten

10. The biggest lie you will ever tell is the one you tell yourself.

I have learned through experience that: "People do what they do because they believe what they believe." That knowledge has been confirmed in my spirit by the words of Solomon given us in Proverbs 23:7 which says:

"As a man thinks in his heart – so is he."

One of the saddest and most destructive things that I have discovered about human behavior is that many times our thoughts, our ideas about life and relationships and the decisions good and bad that we make are initiated by the lies that we have been told and have received as the truth growing up as infants and toddlers and teens and young adults and sadly even some folks who should be old enough to know better. Mean spirited hateful comments thrown about inside a family because of anger or frustration are often received by our children as the truth whether they were meant to or not. Comments like: You were an accident. It would have been better if you had never been born. You are stupid. You can't get anything right. Why can't you be like your sister/brother? You are sorry just like your daddy/mama. Nobody cares what you think. You're never going to amount to anything. I hate you. You make me sick. I wish you were dead. I never want to see you again. You are a loser. I will never forgive you. And when you get a little older you begin to face this kind of lie: One little drink won't hurt you. Come on just take one hit. Nobody is going to know. What they don't know won't hurt them. If you really loved me you would let me…{fill in the blank}. Everybody's doing it.

If you grow up having to carry the baggage of those lies, you could wind up with some serious relationship and behavioral issues.

Our problems dramatically increase when we choose to receive those kinds of lies into our heart, mind, soul and spirit. Choosing to accept the mean-spirited, cruel, disrespectful and demeaning things that we are confronted with throughout the early years of our life begins to engrave upon our hearts a sense of hopelessness, despair, anger, fear, anxiety, worry, lack of trust and failure in every effort and every relationship.

Then it becomes even worse when we begin to "justify" our increasing inability to control our behaviors or when we "fail to take responsibility" for our poor choices in life and relationships. Those justifications I talked about earlier like: "Everybody's doing it." or "What they don't know won't hurt them." or "I'm only hurting myself – I'm not hurting anybody else." Finally, at the end of our rope, we embrace the greatest lie of all – that the only way to stop the pain, the only way to deal with the hurt or anger or frustration or unforgiveness is to numb those feelings with alcohol, drugs and bad relationships. And then we make the saddest and most tragic decision of all. We begin to lie to ourselves about our addictive and out-of-control behaviors. Lies like: "I'm a functional alcoholic. I drink responsibly. I only use drugs recreationally. I can handle my liquor. I'm not hurting anyone if I drink in the privacy of my own home. I'm just a social drinker. I can always get

a friend to be my designated driver. Once an alcoholic –
always an alcoholic. Once a druggie – always a druggie.
Once a pervert – always a pervert. My life is a wreck; it's
always going to be a wreck and there is really nothing I
can do about it so I might as well learn to live with it…"

**OK Pastor, you've shown us the dark side so now why
don't you give us some advice on how to step into the
light of the truth and escape the lies that have
diminished our life.**

Start by getting on your knees somewhere privately and
crying out to your Father in Heaven to give you the
strength, courage and commitment to receive the following
things:

*Pray for a Hunger for His Word

Let Psalm 139:23-24 become the desire of your heart:

*"Search me, O God, and know my heart; test me and know
my anxious thoughts. See if there is any offensive way in
me, and lead me in the way everlasting."*

***Pray for the Faith to define yourself according to who
God's Word says you are and not by who man says you
are. {or even who <u>you</u> say you are}**

In Faith believe Psalm 139:13 – 14 when it says:

*"For you created my inmost being; you knit me together in
my mother's womb. I praise you because I am fearfully and
wonderfully made; your works are wonderful, I know that
full well."*

67

*Rebuke the lie that you have been telling yourself that: Your life is a wreck; it's always going to be a wreck and there is really nothing you can do about it. So, you might as well learn to live with it...

And receive and believe God's Word {instead of man's} when He says to you in Jeremiah 29:11:

"For I know the plans I have for you," declares the Lord, plans to prosper you and not to harm you, plans to give you a hope and a future. Then you will call upon me and come and pray to me, and I will listen to you. You will seek me and find me when you seek me with all your heart. I will be found by you", declares the Lord, "and will bring you back from captivity." I will gather you from all the nations and places where I have banished you," declares the Lord," and will bring you back to the place from which I carried you into exile."

*Pray for GOD to give you the <u>understanding</u>, the <u>strength</u>, the <u>commitment</u> and the <u>love and mercy in your heart</u> to forgive everyone who has ever hurt, disrespected, lied on, abused or misused you in your life.

<u>Understanding</u> – because you must learn that carrying bitterness, anger, hatred, bigotry and revenge in your heart will destroy you long before it destroys those who have hurt you.

<u>Strength</u> - because it is not in man's nature to forgive rather it is man's nature to get even.

<u>Commitment</u> - because forgiveness is a process.

<u>Love and Mercy</u> because it's written that: "Love has forgiven what Mercy Forgot."

*Make a covenant agreement with God and yourself that you will put aside once and for all and forever blaming others for the circumstances you have found yourself in and instead take on complete personal responsibility for the situation you have found yourself in and your plan to change it.

Matthew 7:3-5:

"Why do you look at the speck of sawdust in your brother's eye and pay no attention to the plank in your own eye? How can you say to your brother, let me take the speck out of your eye, when all the time there is a plank in your own eye? You hypocrite, first take the plank out of your own eye, and then you will see clearly to remove the speck from your brother's eye."

*Begin as soon as possible building an intimate, personal, one on one relationship with God through Christ Jesus.

Ephesians 5:8-10 says this:

"for you were once darkness, but now you are light in the Lord. Live as children of light {for the fruit of light consists in all goodness, righteousness and truth} <u>and find out what pleases the Lord."</u>

The only way that I know of to find out what pleases the Lord is:

1. To be in His Word <u>every</u> day, not just reading His Word but studying His Word and praying for Him to reveal Himself to you by the power of His Word through Revelation Knowledge.

2. To be on your knees before Him privately <u>every</u> day in fervent prayer.

3.To find yourself a Bible believing, Holy Ghost filled place of Worship where people are free to worship openly and there is a Pastor there that preaches the Word straight forwardly and truthfully without political correctness.

4. And make a concerted effort to find people to hang out with that love God as much or more than you do.

And I will end this subject this way:

There are 1189 chapters – 31,102 verses and 2,128 pages in the Bible I currently teach from. I didn't wait till I had read the entire Book from cover to cover before I started living for God through Christ Jesus and you shouldn't either. Just pick up your Bible and start reading and the first time you come upon something you are doing that is not pleasing to God --- STOP DOING IT!!! And likewise when you come across something that <u>does</u> please God but you are <u>not</u> doing it--- GET TO DOING IT!!! If you will just do that, by the time you have read all the way through your life will have already begun to take a BIG turn for the better.

Here is an example. Out of the 31,102 verses in God's Word I am going to share just 5 verses with you that if you would just do this, your life would change so radically for the better you would not be able to believe it.

Romans 12:1-2

"Therefore, I urge you, brothers, in view of God's mercy, to offer your bodies as living sacrifices, holy and pleasing to God – this is your spiritual act of worship. Do not conform any longer to the pattern of this world, but be transformed by the renewing of your mind. Then you will be able to test and approve what God's will is – his good pleasing and perfect will."

Hebrews 12:1-3:

"Therefore, since we are surrounded by such a great cloud of witnesses, let us throw off everything that hinders and the sin that so easily entangles, and let us run with perseverance the race marked out for us. Let us fix our eyes on Jesus, the author and perfecter of our faith, who for the joy set before him endured the cross, scorning its shame and sat down at the right hand of the throne of God. Consider him who endured such opposition from sinful men, so that you will not grow weary and lose heart."

If you don't want to read about Him – you don't want to know Him.

If you don't want to pray to Him – you don't want a relationship with Him.

If you don't want to worship Him – you don't want to experience Him.

Lesson Number Eleven

11. The devil is a "trespasser."

Once understood, 1Peter 5:8-9, can become a life changing scripture:

"Be self-controlled and alert. Your enemy the devil prowls around like a roaring lion looking for someone to devour. Resist him, standing firm in the faith..."

Back in the day, I would never miss a weekly episode of the Flip Wilson Comedy Hour. One of the catch phrases that he used on the show often and became famous for was the phrase: "The devil made me do it!" The truth is that that particular phrase has been repeated so many times by so many people over the decades that many of us have actually begun to believe it. There was probably a time when even I believed it and used it as an excuse for my ignorant behaviors. What I have now come to understand and know and firmly believe is that we give the devil entirely too much credit for the evil things we do. Please hear my heart on this!!!

The devil cannot <u>MAKE YOU DO ANYTHING</u>...

The devil is not a <u>perpetrator</u> – he is an <u>instigator</u>...

The devil is not the neighborhood bully. He is like the guy standing over in the dark alleyway that says to you: "PSSST, Hey Bud, got a minute? I've got something I want to show you." You <u>do not</u> have to go into the alleyway and you <u>do not</u> have to listen.

Reminder - James 1:13-15 lays the cards up on the table for us this way:

13 When tempted, no one should say, "God is tempting me." For God cannot be tempted by evil, nor does he tempt anyone; 14 but each person is tempted when they are dragged away <u>by their own evil desire and enticed</u>. 15 Then, after desire has conceived, it gives birth to sin; and sin, when it is full-grown, gives birth to death.

Because of the fall of man in the Garden of Eden we are all born with a natural propensity to sin. The type and depth of that sin will always be intensified in our lives in direct proportion to how deeply the lust of our eyes, the needs of our flesh and the pride of life control our carnal nature and diminish our spirit.

Jeremiah 17:9 confirms that dilemma when it makes this lament:

*9 The heart is deceitful above all things
and beyond cure.
Who can understand it?*

Hold on!!! Understand that that verse is talking about the heart of "MAN" not the "HEART OF GOD". Those verses and many others like them are talking about the "carnal mind" not the "Mind of Christ." It is our deepening desire to please God in everything we do and our covenant commitment to live in Him and for Him daily though Jesus Christ our Lord that will alert us to the danger of those things the devil whispers to us in the alleyways of life.

That is why God leaves us without excuse concerning falling to temptation when He says in 1 Corinthians 10:12-13:

12 So, if you think you are standing firm, be careful that you don't fall! 13 No temptation has overtaken you except what is common to mankind. And God is faithful; <u>he will not let you be tempted beyond what you can bear</u>. But when you are tempted, he will also provide a way out so that you can endure it.

Ok, Brother Charlie, if God won't let us "be tempted beyond what we can bear" why am I so often and so easily tempted?

Once again I remind you: It's because you choose <u>NOT</u> to bear it!!!

Brothers and Sisters understand and believe this powerful truth and it will set you free. "The devil is a trespasser but <u>YOU</u> are the blood bought private property of Jesus Christ who bought and paid for you on the cross of Calvary."

THEREFORE....

He has absolutely no authority in your heart, your mind, your marriage, your family or your life – except what <u>YOU</u> give him.

Let me see if I can give you a worldly example of what I am talking about.

My wife and I live in a beautiful little one bedroom log cabin house plopped down in the middle of nine acres of gorgeous pine and polar trees. I can sit on my front porch and look out across a beautiful five acre lake framed in white water lilies and watch those big bass and bream stirring the water. Sadly, around the perimeter of that beautiful lake I have had to post signs about every hundred feet that say: NO TRESPASSING-SURVIVORS WILL BE PROSECUTED! – to keep unwanted visitors away from my lake. Now, let's imagine for a moment that I am sitting on that same front porch and suddenly a stranger pulls up in his pickup truck pulling his boat behind it. He then proceeds to put his boat along with his bait and tackle into my lake, row out to the center and begin catching my bass and my bream. Now imagine that I just sit on my porch in amazement at what is happening but say nothing to the intruder. Later I watched him load up his boat, his gear and my fish and leave. Then imagine the next day the same man returns with one of his friends and they both spend the afternoon fishing in my pond-catching my fish. And once again I say nothing. Now comes the third day and the same man comes once again this time with two of his friends. Finally I have had enough. I rise to my feet, walk down the hill to the lakeside and confront the trespasser. "Hey Jack, didn't you see the trespassing signs that I have posted around this lake about every hundred feet?" And now guess what the intruder says, "Trespassing signs? What trespassing signs?" Pointing down the tree line I exclaim, "Those trespassing signs nailed to those trees along the road there!"

OK, Hold on! Here it comes! Here is what happens!

And then the trespasser says: "I saw the trespassing signs, but when I pulled in with my boat and pushed out in the lake, I saw you sitting on the front porch watching me fish and you didn't say or do anything. The next day when I came back with my friend and you watched us fish but you didn't say or do anything. And then today when I came back with two of my friends, I thought it was going to be okay because you never said or did anything about my being here on your private property, fishing in your pond."

That's the way the devil thinks. He can clearly see the "posted signs" placed all around you by the Blood of Christ but he will trespass anyway hoping you will say and do nothing about it. If you do not "resist him standing firm in the faith" every time he comes around, he will trespass on you as often as he can.

OK, here is the big question. Come on men, If you came home from a hard day at work, walked into your house and found an intruder sitting on your couch with his arm around your wife, ordering your kids around and eating your milk and cookies, I guarantee you, you would immediately begin to take matters into your own hands. If you didn't immediately snatch him up by the neck, whip him within an inch of his life and boot him out the front door, you would at least confront him verbally in such a way that he knew without any doubt that he had better depart the area - and quickly! Something like: "Hey Jack! You have no business in my house. That's <u>MY</u> wife you've got your arm around; you have no authority over my kids and you are dang sure not welcome to my cookies and milk. I was savin' those for when I got home from work tonight. You have about two seconds to get your butt up and get out of my house before I call the authorities to take you out!!!{the authorities being the Swat Team}"

If you know that's what the flesh and blood man should do, then why don't you think that's what the Spirit man should do? When the devil shows up in your house, your marriage, your family or your life - REBUKE THAT SUCKER!!! Shake your finger in his face in Jesus Name. Tell him he is trespassing and that he's got about two seconds to clear the area before you call the authorities to take him out {the authorities in this case being the Father, the Son and the Holy Spirit}.

James 4:7-8 reminds us:

⁷ Submit yourselves, then, to God. Resist the devil, and he will flee from you. ⁸ Come near to God and he will come near to you. Wash your hands, you sinners, and purify your hearts, you double-minded.

I want to take just a few more minutes before we move on to the next Life Lesson to give you one last {but very important} insight into the devices of the devil. Once you understand the methods {which are few} of his madness, you can be much better prepared to defeat him in the "alleyways" of life.

I have already told you about the little cabin on the lake where my wife and I live, so, it probably wouldn't be very hard for you to figure out that I love fishing. I love to go fishing because it is enjoyable and getting a fish to find himself hooked, reeled in, gutted, filleted, fried and on my plate is a fairly simple matter and requires very little knowledge and not much equipment. I have learned through experience that it doesn't take much to make a fish succumb to "temptation" or as we say "bite." I know that the <u>enticement</u> must be right. But, experience has taught me that I only need to take a few always successful types of bait with me in my tackle box to have a successful day of fishing {tempting}. All I need is seven old standbys that have worked for me every time - and a little bit of patience. Those old standbys are: a Jitterbug, a Hula Popper, a Broken Minnow, a Jig, a Plastic Worm, some Night Crawlers and some Crickets.

The devil is also a master fisherman who takes great delight in finding ways to sink his hooks into us and drag us into the boat of eternal damnation. He too understands that the conditions must be right and he must be patient in order to prevail. He also understands that the enticements must be right. Thousands of years of experience have taught the devil that <u>he also</u> only needs seven old standbys in his "tackle box" to have a successful day of destroying the hopes and futures of God's children. And they are: doubt, deceit, needs of the flesh, lust of the eyes, pride of life, rebellion and denial. He tried them first in the Garden of Eden:

Genesis 3:1-7: The Fall

¹ Now the serpent was more crafty than any of the wild animals the LORD God had made. He said to the woman, "Did God really say, 'You must not eat from any tree in the garden'?" {DOUBT}

² The woman said to the serpent, "We may eat fruit from the trees in the garden, ³ but God did say, 'You must not eat fruit from the tree that is in the middle of the garden, and you must not touch it, or you will die.'"

4 "You will not certainly die," the serpent said to the woman. 5 "For God knows that when you eat from it your eyes will be opened, and you will be like God, knowing good and evil." {DECEIT}

6 When the woman saw that the fruit of the tree was good for food {NEEDS OF THE FLESH} and pleasing to the eye {LUST OF THE EYES}, and also desirable for gaining wisdom {PRIDE OF LIFE}, she took some and ate it. She also gave some to her husband, who was with her, and he ate it {REBELLION}. 7 Then the eyes of both of them were opened, and they realized they were naked; so they sewed fig leaves together and made coverings for themselves {DENIAL}

And because those old standbys work so well, Satan has been using them every since. Satan has become so confidently arrogant using his time tested approach to temptation that he even tried to use it on Christ for forty days and forty nights in the desert.

Luke 4: Jesus Is Tested in the Wilderness

1 Jesus, full of the Holy Spirit, left the Jordan and was led by the Spirit into the wilderness, 2 where for forty days he was tempted by the devil. He ate nothing during those days, and at the end of them he was hungry.{THE CONDITIONS WERE RIGHT AND SATAN THOUGHT HE HAD THE ENTICEMENTS TO PREVAIL*}*

3 The devil said to him, "If you are the Son of God {DOUBT}, tell this stone to become bread."

⁴ Jesus answered, "It is written: 'Man shall not live on bread alone.'{THE REBUKE}

⁵ The devil led him up to a high place and showed him in an instant all the kingdoms of the world. ⁶ And he said to him, "I will give you all their authority and splendor; it has been given to me, and I can give it to anyone I want to. ⁷ If you worship me, it will all be yours."{LUST OF THE EYES}

⁸ Jesus answered, "It is written: 'Worship the Lord your God and serve him only.'{ANOTHER REBUKE}

⁹ The devil led him to Jerusalem and had him stand on the highest point of the temple. "If you are the Son of God {DOUBT}," he said, "throw yourself down from here. ¹⁰ For it is written:

*"'He will command his angels concerning you to guard you carefully;
¹¹ they will lift you up in their hands, so that you will not strike your foot against a stone.'{PRIDE OF LIFE}*

¹² Jesus answered, "It is said: 'Do not put the Lord your God to the test.'{A FINAL REBUKE}

¹³ When the devil had finished all this tempting,

he left him until a more opportune time!!!

Pay attention to that last verse and learn and understand from it that the devil will never give up on trying to trip you up. The more you love God the more the devil is determined to destroy you –REBUKE HIM!!!

Life Lesson Number Twelve

12. If I always thank God for the little things, He will always bless me with greater things

How often do you find yourself down on your knees just thanking God for the "little things"- those things that we just constantly take for granted? If you're like most folks you probably don't spend much time on your knees unless you're in a crisis or need something you think no man can provide. It was my self-sufficient attitude rooted deeply in my arrogance and pride that caused me to always give myself complete credit for every good thing that happened to me in life and to always blame someone else for the bad things that happened. I had to learn the hard way through the power of God's Word, that the key to the greater blessings of God coming down into my life were directly proportionate to the amount of Thanksgiving I was sending up to heaven for the "little things". This sound biblical principle of living is no better demonstrated anywhere in God's word than in a story called "The feeding of the 5000". What I find remarkable about this principle is that it validated not in just one book of the Bible but all four Gospels – in Matthew 14:19-21, Mark 6:37-44, Luke 9:12-17 and John 6:11. Check out how each of these disciples describes this event exactly the same way.

Matthew 14:19-21 {Jesus Feeds the Five Thousand}

13 When Jesus heard what had happened, he withdrew by boat privately to a solitary place. Hearing of this, the crowds followed him on foot from the towns. 14 When Jesus landed and saw a large crowd, he had compassion on them and healed their sick.

¹⁵ As evening approached, the disciples came to him and said, "This is a remote place, and it's already getting late. Send the crowds away, so they can go to the villages and buy themselves some food."

¹⁶ Jesus replied, "They do not need to go away. You give them something to eat."

¹⁷ "We have here only five loaves of bread and two fish," they answered.

*¹⁸ "Bring them here to me," he said. ¹⁹ And he directed the people to sit down on the grass. **Taking the five loaves and the two fish and looking up to heaven, he gave thanks and broke the loaves.** Then he gave them to the disciples, and the disciples gave them to the people. ²⁰ They all ate and were satisfied, **and the disciples picked up twelve basketfuls of broken pieces that were left over.** ²¹ The number of those who ate was about five thousand men, besides women and children.*

Mark 6:37-44 {Jesus Feeds the Five Thousand}

³⁷ But he answered, "You give them something to eat."

They said to him, "That would take more than half a year's wages! Are we to go and spend that much on bread and give it to them to eat?"

[38] *"How many loaves do you have?" he asked. "Go and see."*

When they found out, they said, "Five—and two fish."

[39] *Then Jesus directed them to have all the people sit down in groups on the green grass.* [40] *So they sat down in groups of hundreds and fifties.* [41] **Taking the five loaves and the two fish and looking up to heaven, he gave thanks and broke the loaves.** *Then he gave them to his disciples to distribute to the people. He also divided the two fish among them all.* [42] **They all ate and were satisfied,** [43] **and the disciples picked up twelve basketfuls of broken pieces of bread and fish.{that were left over}** [44] *The number of the men who had eaten was five thousand.*

Luke 9:12-17 {Jesus Feeds the Five Thousand}

[12] *Late in the afternoon the Twelve came to him and said, "Send the crowd away so they can go to the surrounding villages and countryside and find food and lodging, because we are in a remote place here."*

[13] *He replied, "You give them something to eat."*

They answered, "We have only five loaves of bread and two fish—unless we go and buy food for all this crowd." [14] *(About five thousand men were there.)*

But he said to his disciples, "Have them sit down in groups of about fifty each." [15] *The disciples did so, and everyone sat down.* [16] **Taking the five loaves and the two fish and looking up to heaven, he gave thanks and broke them.** *Then he gave them to the disciples to distribute to the* *people.* **<u>*¹⁷ They all ate and were satisfied, and the disciples picked up twelve basketfuls of broken pieces that were left over.*</u>**

John 6:5-13 {Jesus Feeds the Five Thousand}

⁵ When Jesus looked up and saw a great crowd coming toward him, he said to Philip, "Where shall we buy bread for these people to eat?" ⁶ He asked this only to test him, for he already had in mind what he was going to do.

⁷ Philip answered him, "It would take more than half a year's wages to buy enough bread for each one to have a bite!"

⁸ Another of his disciples, Andrew, Simon Peter's brother, spoke up, ⁹ "Here is a boy with five small barley loaves and two small fish, but how far will they go among so many?"

¹⁰ Jesus said, "Have the people sit down." There was plenty of grass in that place, and they sat down (about five thousand men were there). ¹¹ **<u>*Jesus then took the loaves, gave thanks, and distributed to those who were seated as much as they wanted. He did the same with the fish.*</u>**

¹² When they had all had enough to eat, he said to his disciples, "Gather the pieces that are left over. Let nothing be wasted." ¹³ **<u>*So they gathered them and filled twelve baskets with the pieces of the five barley loaves left over by those who had eaten.*</u>**

If that were you and me and Christ had turned and pointed to the five thousand men and their wives and children and said: "You feed them!" We would have had the same attitude they did and we would be saying, "Are you crazy Jesus?" We would have told the little boy who ran up and offered all he had {two fish and a few barley loaves} – "Boy, we can't feed all these people with a couple of boney fish and a few pieces of bread. Get back over there with your mama and sit down. Are you stupid?"

BUT THAT'S NOT WHAT OUR SAVIOR DID. HE SHOWED US A KINGDOM SECRET ABOUT HOW TO RECEIVE MIRACULOUS BLESSINGS. HE LIFTED UP THE TWO BONEY FISH AND THE FEW BARLEY LOAVES AND SAID – THANK YOU LORD FOR THE BLESSING. AND NOT ONLY DID GOD RESPOND BY ALLOWING EVERYONE TO BE FED AS MUCH AS THEY WANTED - BUT – THERE WERE <u>LEFTOVERS</u>!!!

We need to get this folks. When we have a thankful heart toward God Almighty, He is not only going to give us all we need, but His blessings will become so abundant, we will have LEFTOVERS.

That's why God's Word says in <u>1 Corinthians 2:9</u> :

No eye has seen, no ear has heard, and no human mind has conceived"— the things that God has prepared for those who love him—

Understand that thanking God every day for the little things is just one of the many "secrets of the kingdom" that are given us throughout the Bible.

In Matthew 13:11-12 Christ says this:

[1] "...the knowledge of the secrets of the kingdom of heaven has been given to you , but not to them. [12] Whoever has will be given more, and they will have an abundance. But whoever does not have, even what they have will be taken from them.

I have learned the hard way that those who always have a thankful heart for the little things God has provided and are truly thankful for them will reap an abundance of further blessing. But those of us who are not thankful for the little things we have now – even that will be taken from us.

Not long ago as I pondered on this truth and I penned these thoughts:

When the light of a new day falls across my bed in the early morning hours and my slowly awakening consciousness allows me to understand that God has given me another day to get it right – should I pray a prayer of thanksgiving.

When my feet feel the coolness of my bedroom floor as I stretch my still healthy body and begin to plan the events of the day with a sound and sober mind – that is when I should pray a prayer of thanksgiving.

As I sink into my easy chair in the comfort and safety of my living room, drink my first sip of coffee and watch on my television the images of a world wracked with hate and bigotry and prejudice and unkindness and un-forgiveness, but can still believe in faith that my God is in control – should I pray a prayer of thanksgiving.

When I take my beautiful and faithful wife and my arms and kiss her goodbye and tell her that I love her as I start out the door toward the job that provides for us – should I pray a prayer of thanksgiving.

When I start home at the end of the day knowing that my presence in the workplace and in this world has somehow made today better because I was able to focus on the needs of others instead of myself – should I pray a prayer of thanksgiving.

When I sit down at the dinner table in fellowship with the beautiful family I have been given and enjoy the delicious meal that has been provided and prepared for our nourishment – should I pray a prayer of thanksgiving.

When I purpose to turn on the television and find a program to relax and watch and discover that there is nothing before me worth watching so I turn instead to the comfort of God's word and his covenant promises – should I pray a prayer of thanksgiving.

When I climb between the cool sheets on this warm summer night, nestled down into the comfort of my soft mattress, safe and at peace, with the one who has been, and is, and always will be, the love of my life at my side and feel the hope that God will give me another tomorrow to get it right again – should I pray a prayer of thanksgiving.

***Finally I have come to the place in my life where my answer to those questions is a resounding YES. Because my friend I have discovered by experience that for every prayer of Thanksgiving that goes up in gratefulness for "just the little things", rivers of blessing flow back from the Gates of Heaven. And that on the other side of every trial and every temptation there is always a blessing.

Life Lesson Number Thirteen

13. The consequences of my life are not left to "chance" but rather to <u>CHOICE</u>.

There is an old saying: "If it wasn't for bad luck, I wouldn't have no luck at all." The truth is that the consequences that we find ourselves in have absolutely nothing to do with "chance" and everything to do with "choice."

Deuteronomy 30:19-20 says this:

This day I [19] call the heavens and the earth as witnesses against you that I have set before you life and death, blessings and curses. Now choose life, so that you and your children may live and that you may love the Lord your God, listen to his voice and hold fast to him. For the Lord is your life...

CHOICE!!! Why in the world did God create us with the ability and even the freedom to make choices in our life? Wouldn't life be a lot simpler if He had created us where we <u>HAD</u> to obey Him and <u>HAD</u> to love Him with no choice in the matter? YES, it might have been easier BUT it would not have given us the opportunity to truthfully demonstrate two of God's most desired behaviors in our relationship with Him.

Those two behaviors are: Unconditional Love <u>for</u> Him and Unquestionable Obedience <u>to</u> Him.

Even the very first Man and Woman created by God and placed in a situation in a Paradise that you and I could only dream of – with every possible provision and amenity and authority they could ever want - could not demonstrate the Love and Obedience needed to allow them to choose to refrain from the one and only thing God commanded them NOT to do. REMEMBER ?

Genesis 2:15-17:

[15] The LORD God took the man and put him in the Garden of Eden to work it and take care of it. [16] And the LORD God commanded the man, "You are free to eat from any tree in the garden; [17] but you must not eat from the tree of the knowledge of good and evil, for when you eat from it you will certainly die."

Yep! They ate it.

That initial unfortunate disobedience of Adam and Eve has flowed down generationally to all of mankind. And for that very reason we are all born with a natural propensity to sin and the curse of having to live through the consequences of the good or bad choices we make in life. There is a HUGE life lesson in God's Word for all of us concerning how God reacts to us when we make poor and ungodly choices in our life and then try to blame the disastrous results of these choices on other people or circumstances. Check out God's handling of the Adam's and Eve's and the Serpent's disobedience and their subsequent excuses for their behavior as written in Genesis 3:11-19:

[11] And God said, "...Have you eaten from the tree that I commanded you not to eat from?"

¹² The man said, "__That woman you put here with me__—she gave me some fruit from the tree, and I ate it."

Oh, yea Adam, it's not your fault – it's that woman's fault. Wait a minute! Weren't you still alone in the garden when God came and instructed you not to eat of the fruit of the tree of the knowledge of good and evil? Yep! And I'm quite sure Adam that since God made it patently clear that if you did – you would die; you probably filled Eve in on that important piece of information not long after God presented her to you. Oh! and Adam, when you saw her picking the fruit, why didn't you immediately exclaim: Eve, are you crazy? I told you God said not to mess with the fruit on that tree. Oh and one last thing Adam – When she offered it to you, why in the heck did you take it? I don't think God's buyin' it – Adam.

¹³ Then the LORD God said to the woman, "What is this you have done?"
The woman said, "__The serpent deceived me__, and I ate."

Congratulations Eve – we can now give you full credit for being the first person in all of creation to coin the phase and thereby use the aforementioned excuse: "The Devil made me do it." You knew God asked you not to do it. BUT driven by the needs of your flesh, the lust of your eyes and pride you did it anyway. And so have I and so has every living human being on this planet in one way or another. So let's prepare ourselves to suffer the consequences that not even the Serpent escaped.

¹⁴ __So the LORD God said to the serpent__,
"Because you have done this,

92

"Cursed are you above all livestock
and all wild animals!
You will crawl on your belly
and you will eat dust
all the days of your life.
¹⁵ And I will put enmity
between you and the woman,
and between your offspring and hers;
he will crush your head,
and you will strike his heel."
*¹⁶ **To the woman he said,***
"I will make your pains in childbearing very severe;
with painful labor you will give birth to children.
Your desire will be for your husband,
and he will rule over you."
*¹⁷ **To Adam he said,***
"Because you listened to your wife and ate fruit from the
tree about which I commanded you, 'You must not eat from
it,'
"Cursed is the ground because of you;
through painful toil you will eat food from it
all the days of your life.
¹⁸ It will produce thorns and thistles for you,
and you will eat the plants of the field.
¹⁹ By the sweat of your brow
you will eat your food
until you return to the ground,
since from it you were taken;
for dust you are
and to dust you will return."

So the LORD God said to the serpent...
To the woman he said...

Do you see the pattern forming? God holds each one of us personally and individually accountable for the bad choices we make in life and He allows the consequences that go with that poor choice. He does not respond well to excuses or blaming others. He only responds to confession and repentance. Unfortunately in the case of the Garden of Eden – no confession – no repentance – no taking responsibility – just excuses. If that's the way you have been living your life I urge you to make a course correction today.

Choose today to humble yourself before God and do this:

*Take full responsibility for the poor choices you have made in life without excuse.
*Confess them and ask God to forgive you for them.
*THEN – Repent of them! {The Word says "REPENT and be saved" - not "confess and be saved"}
*Press in to read and study and apply the "Sound Biblical Principles of Living" outlined in God's Word – particularly those principles outlined so clearly by Christ Himself in the New Testament writings of Matthew, Mark, Luke and John.
*And engrave on your heart forever these powerful choices laid before you every single day for the rest of your life:

Deuteronomy 30:15-16:

[15] See, I set before you today life and prosperity, death and destruction. [16] For I command you today to love the LORD your God, to walk in obedience to him, and to keep his

commands, decrees and laws; then you will live and increase, and the LORD your God will bless you in the land you are entering to possess.

And Proverbs 8:10 which urges us to:

"Choose God's instruction over silver and His knowledge instead of gold."

And again in Proverbs 12:26 which reminds us that:

"The righteous choose their friends carefully, but the way of the wicked leads them astray."

And finally engrave this on your heart as well from James 4:4 which warns:

"You adulterous people, don't you know that friendship with the world means enmity against God? Therefore, anyone who chooses to be a friend of the world becomes an enemy of God."

Life Lesson Number Fourteen

14. Success in life is not determined by what you have done – rather it is determined by what you have done ABOUT what you have done.

Knowing without doubt that God was calling me into the Ministry, I still found myself wallowing in the misery and regret of my life before I met Christ and chose to live for and in Him and no longer live for and in the world. One day I was whining and belly aching about: "How could God ever use somebody like me – that had lived the messed up life I had lived?"

Still ringing in my heart, mind, soul and spirit until this day is a Pastor's strong rebuke of my complaint. He looked straight into my eyes and said:

"Listen to me Charlie Haynes; don't you EVER allow the sin of your past to stand in the way of your future with Christ. The sin in your past DOES NOT define you in God's eyes. It is something you DID – it is NOT who you are."

"You are who God Almighty says you are – not who or what someone else says you are. If you think you would be the first jacked up, misguided man in all of creation that God ever used to do miraculous works – you would be sadly mistaken. Go get your Bible son. Turn to the book of Acts and read about a man named Saul – I think the facts about HIS journey will encourage you."

I am so glad that I decided to follow that Pastors advice!

Saul was recognized by his peers as one of the most educated and informed Bible scholars of his day – trained by the great teacher of the law, Gamaliel. However, Saul had become a zealot or in other words a religious fanatic of his day. Although Saul believed in God, he fully, faithfully and fiercely believed that Jesus Christ was a false Messiah and that Christianity was a false and dangerous movement. The first time that we meet Saul in the Bible is in the book of Acts Chapter 7 Verse 58 and following where we see him joining in, overseeing and approving the stoning death of one of Christ's disciples named Stephen. On the heels of that event starting in Acts Chapter 8 we watch Saul embark on a murderous rampage. Armed with letters of authority given by local religious leaders, he began rounding up all the followers of Christ he could find and turning them over to be imprisoned, tortured and murdered.

It was while he was on such a quest along the Damascus Road that he had a life changing encounter. Suddenly as he neared Damascus, a light from Heaven shone around him that was so bright and so powerful that it literally knocked him off the horse he was riding onto the ground below and he heard a voice say to him:

"Saul – Saul, why do you persecute me?"

"Who are you, Lord?" Saul asked. "I am Jesus who you are persecuting," He said. "Now get up and go into the city and you will be told what you must do."

Saul got up from the ground, but when he opened his eyes he could see nothing. He had been blinded by the light. So they had to lead him by the hand to a house in the city of

Damascus where for three days he remained blinded and neither ate nor drank anything. The Word further tells us that there was a disciple of Christ living in Damascus named Ananias. The Lord called Ananias in a vision and told him to go to a house on Straight Street and ask for a man from Tarsus named Saul – you will find him there praying. And the Lord said, I have also shown Saul a vision that a man named Ananias will come and by "a laying on of hands" will restore his sight. The Word tells us that Ananias was very hesitant to do what the Lord had asked him. And he said, "Lord I have heard about this man and all the harm he has done to your holy people in Jerusalem. And I heard he has come here with authority from the chief priest to arrest all who call on the name of Christ."

And then God said something to Ananias that you and I might find incredible and unbelievable. The Lord said to Ananias, Go! This man is my "**chosen instrument**" to proclaim my name to the Gentiles and their Kings and all the people of Israel. I will show him how much he must suffer for My Name.

So Ananias went to the house and entered it. Placing his hands on Saul, he told him that Christ Jesus who appeared to him on the road has sent me so that you may see again and be filled with the Holy Spirit. And immediately, something like scales fell from Saul eyes and he could see again. Saul got up and was baptized, and after taking some food, he regained his strength.

And what the Word tells us happened next is even more amazing.

Saul spent the next several days with Christ's disciples in Damascus. And then at once began to preach in the synagogues that Jesus is the Son of God. All those who saw him were astonished because they knew the kind of man Saul once was. Saul's conversion {more correctly his transformation} was made complete when he began to preach Christ crucified.

And by the Lord's decree Saul, the religious fanatic, persecutor and murderer of the followers of Christ became Paul, the Apostle of Christ and author of much of the New Testament we read and study today. Paul – a man whose transformation was so miraculous that this so called brilliant Bible scholar and Christian hater said later in 1Corinthians 2:1-5:

"And so it was with me brothers and sisters, that when I came to you I did not come with eloquence or human wisdom as I proclaim to you my testimony about God. For I resolved to know nothing while I was with you except Jesus Christ and him crucified. I came to you in weakness and with great fear and trembling my message and my preaching were not with wise and persuasive words, but with a demonstration of the Holy Spirit's power, so that your faith might not rest on human wisdom, but on God's power."

Now that my friends is what I call a "turnaround."

His leadership, his influence, and his legacy led to the formation of many communities dominated by gentile groups that worshiped Jesus and adhered to the Judaic moral code. Paul taught the life and works of Jesus Christ and Christ's teaching of the new covenant (New

Testament) concerning death and resurrection. Fourteen of the 27 books in the New Testament have been attributed to Paul and approximately half of the Book of Acts deals with Paul's life and works. Among all other apostles and missionaries involved in the spread of the Christian faith, Paul's influence on Christian thought and practice has been characterized as being "as profound as it is pervasive."

Ok, so guess what I have learned?

I learned that God had a plan for Saul/Paul before he was knit in his mother's womb. The problem was that Saul was not walking out that plan – BUT – God was never going to give up on the plan. And though the consequences of Saul's actions were painful and hard to go through, going through them helped him {literally} "see the Light" and step into the real purpose God had created him for.

And you know what? I am no different and you are no different either. God had a plan for my life and for over fifty years {like Saul} I thought I had it all figured out and did it my way. But thank God in a moment of desperation and heartbreak, I finally saw "the Light."

After living most of my adult life like I was "going to hell in a handbasket," I finally got knocked off of my high horse by the blinding light of revelation. A revelation shown to me through the love of Christ as a result of the consequences that I had found myself in due to the sin in my life.

I have heard the voice of Christ saying, "Charlie Haynes, WHY do you persecute Me?"

I have stumbled to my feet in the wake of His awesome rebuke only to find myself feeling blinded, helpless, alone and hopeless. {Have you ever been there?}

I have sat alone in the dark for days praying to God for forgiveness. {Have you ever been there?}

Just like Saul, I have received the prayers of comfort and healing of those He sent to minister to me. {Have you ever been there?}

I have shaken my head in amazement and wonder as I heard the voice of Christ confirm in me – Charlie Haynes, you are my chosen instrument to carry my name before the broken, the hopeless, the addicted, the depraved and the deprived on the streets and in the alleyways of this nation; and to carry this word to my church: "Thus says Christ Jesus our Lord, my food is to do the will of him who sent me and to finish His work... I tell you, open your eyes and look at the fields. They are ripe for the harvest."

Please believe me and believe God's Word when it says you were born into this world with a destiny; a destiny that was purposed before you were knit in your mother's womb. God is patiently waiting for you to decide to step into that destiny in Christ so that he may make you another of his chosen instruments to accomplish what he brought you into this world to do.

So then there remains the final question of this chapter.

How can I be used as a "chosen instrument" of God?

*Understand that your sinful behavior DOES NOT disqualify you from being used of God to do miraculous works. (No matter how dark, how dishonest, how sick, how depraved, how perverted or how to totally unacceptable it has been)

*Allow Christ to shine the light of His truth on your life and literally "knock you off your high horse." (i.e. your pedestal)

*Blind your eyes to the things of the world and open them only to the things of God.

*Find yourself often down on your knees crying out to God through Christ Jesus to forgive your sins against him and then repent of them.

*Receive Christ Jesus as Lord of your life (that is give Him complete authority over your life) and believe in faith that He is the risen Savior.

*Follow in the Waters of Baptism – Baptized in the name of the Father and the Son and the Holy Spirit.

*Remember and believe in faith that, in your hour of brokenness and despair God is always prepared to send someone alongside to comfort you.

*Believe and receive that God, before you were knit in your mother's womb, already had a purpose and plan for your life and that if you are still breathing – plan the is still on the table.

*And finally, remember that living for Christ and obeying the commands of God will require faith, perseverance, suffering and sacrifice. But the eternal reward that follows that – is joy beyond human imagination.

Because I have chosen to live by these principles I stand before you today fully understanding and celebrating those same words so gratefully spoken by the apostle Paul (once known as Saul) when he said in 1Timothy 1:12-16:

"I thank Christ Jesus our Lord, who has given me strength, that he considered me faithful, of pointing me to His service. Even though I was once a blasphemer and a persecutor and a violent man, I was shown mercy because I acted in ignorance and unbelief. The grace of our Lord was poured out on me abundantly, along with the faith and love that are in Christ Jesus. Here is a trustworthy saying that deserves full acceptance: Christ Jesus came into the world to save sinners – of whom I am the worst. But for that very reason I was shown mercy so that in me, the worst of sinners, Christ Jesus might display his unlimited patience as an example for those who would believe on Him and receive eternal life."

Life Lesson Number Fifteen

15. Salvation is a "PROCESS"

Salvation is not a "free ride" to Heaven and Jesus Christ is not a "ticket agent" sent by God to "punch your ticket."

You don't accept Christ as Lord of your life and then there's a big "poof" and a "puff of smoke" and "TAA DAA!!" You're a Saint and the whole rest of your life becomes a "bowl of cherries".

That's why God's Word is full of scriptures like:

"Therefore my dear friends, as you have always obeyed – not only in my presence, but now much more in my absence – <u>*continue to work out your salvation with fear and trembling,*</u> *for it is God who works in you to will and to act according to his good purpose. Do everything without complaining or arguing, so that you may become blameless and pure, children of God without fault in a crooked and depraved generation.* {Philippians Chapter 2:12-15}*

"If they have escaped the corruption of the world by knowing our Lord and Savior Jesus Christ and are again entangled in it and overcome, they are worse off at the end than they were at the beginning. It would have been better for them not to have known the way of righteousness then to have known it and then turn their backs on the sacred command that was passed on to them. Of them the Proverbs are true: a dog returns to his vomit and a sow that is washed goes back to her wallowing in the mud." {2Peter 2:20-22}

The Lord says: "These people come near to me with their mouth and honor me with their lips, but their hearts are far from me. Their worship of me is made up only of rules taught by men." {Isaiah 29:13}

"Woe to you, teachers of the law and the Pharisees, you hypocrites! You travel over land and sea to win a single convert, and when he becomes one you make him twice as much a son of hell as you are." {Matthew 23:15}

And what about this commitment called for in Luke 9:23.....

Then Christ said to them all: "If anyone would come after me, he must <u>deny himself</u> and take up <u>his cross</u> and follow me."

Coming to <u>TRULY</u> "know" Christ so that you can actually be Christ-like takes a great deal of faith and obedience and perseverance and strength of character.   {Not your character – HIS CHARACTER}

Most people, when asked if they are Christians and say yes actually mean "I am an American". {America is considered to be a Christian nation therefore I consider myself a Christian} Also most people when asked if they "know" who someone is and say yes, actually mean I have "heard" of them. The definition "to know" is: to have all the facts about something or someone and be certain the facts are true – to have true information about – to have firmly in mind – to have an understanding, information or knowledge of – to have experience with – to recognize – to be able to tell apart from others. The Biblical definition is: to know <u>intimately</u> and <u>absolutely</u>.

In John1: 26 – 27 we hear John the Baptist say to the church leaders of his day:

"I baptize with water, but among you stands one <u>you do not know</u>. He is the one who comes after me the thongs of whose sandals I am not worthy to untie."

I can think of at least twelve steps I will have taken in my life before I can truthfully say that I "KNOW" Jesus Christ and that I have truly "walked out my Salvation." Maybe there are more steps but here are mine.

Twelve Steps to "KNOWING" Jesus

Step 1.Hearing about Him…It would be difficult for me to believe that there is anyone in the United States of America {or most of the planet} from kindergarten to adult that hasn't "heard of" Jesus Christ – whether it was from someone who was constantly "dropping" His name to establish their religiosity or from someone who included his name in an angry outburst of profanity or from someone preaching about Him on radio or television or the internet or in church. But my experience has been that the only true way to "hear about Him" <u>IN TRUTH</u> is by getting in your BIBLE and reading about Him for yourself. Bible reading exposes you to the opportunity to read about Christ from the inerrant truth about Him from the Holy Spirit inspired Word of God.

Romans 10:17 reminds us that, *"Faith comes by hearing and hearing by the word of God."*

There are many effective Bible reading plans available – plans that can help you read through the entire Bible in as

106

little as 90 days. There are also six month and 12 month reading plans available. You can find them at your local Bible bookstore in your community or at an online store. Whatever plan you choose make sure that you are in the Word every single day.

Daily Bible reading is important but to really know Christ Jesus, <u>Bible study</u> in addition to the reading is critical. Find a place you can settle down comfortably with your Bible for study. In addition get yourself a Concordance that is compatible with the Bible translation you are reading. In addition to that add an illustrated Bible dictionary and a Webster's dictionary to help you research those things you encounter that are not clear to you. There is also a particular type of Bible called a Life Application Bible that is available from any Bible bookstore. These life application Bible's come in most translations and have spectacular study notes at the bottom of each page that help you fully understand the verses above.

And finally, there is the importance of reading and studying your Bible to receive "revelation knowledge" given to you by the Holy Spirit of God while you are reading and studying.

Listen to this awesome exchange between Christ and His disciple Simon Peter in Matthew 16:13 – 19.

*When Jesus came to the region of Caesarea Philippi, he asked his disciples, "Who do people say the Son of Man is?" They replied, "Some say John the Baptist; others say Elijah; and still others, Jeremiah or one of the prophets." "But what about **YOU**?" He asked. "Who do **YOU** say I* *am?" And Simon Peter answered, "You are the Messiah, the Son of the living God."*

Jesus replied, "Blessed are you, Simon son of Jonah, for this was not "REVEALED" to you by flesh and blood, but by my Father in Heaven. And I tell you that you are Peter, and on this rock I will build my church, and the gates of Hell will not overcome it. I will give you the keys to the Kingdom of Heaven; whatever you bind on earth will be bound in Heaven, and whatever you loose on earth will be loosed in heaven."

There is no doubt in my mind that Simon Peter was "the rock" that began the Christian movement during the New Testament times chronicled in the Book of Acts. But I also personally hold that it was the gift of revelation knowledge pointed to by Christ in those Scriptures that qualified Peter to be called "the rock."

Make it a habit to never sit down and open your Bible to read or study it that you do not first bow your head in prayer and ask God to reveal Himself to you through the power of his Word. I promise you - you will not be disappointed.

Step 2.Finding out about him... Jeremiah 29:11 talks about God's promised plan for our life when it says:

"For I know the plans I have for you, declares the Lord, plans to prosper you and not to harm you, plans to give you a hope and a future."

If you have lived a life of disappointment and heartbreak and bad choices and hopelessness as I did, then once you receive and believe and understand the power of that promise, you will gain the desire to go looking for Christ.

In 2 Chronicles 7:14 – 15 the Word gives us this hope:

"If my people, who are called by my name, will humble themselves and pray and seek my face and turn from their wicked ways, then I will hear from Heaven, and I will forgive their sin and will heal their land {life, marriage, family and relationships}." Then my eyes will be opened and my ears attentive to the prayers offered in this place."

Step 3. Seeking Him... In Luke 11:9 Christ Jesus extends this invitation:

"So I say to you: ask and it will be given to you; seek and you will find; knock and the door will be open to you."

Okay, Brother Charlie, how do I do that?

*Build and sustain a habit of reading and studying your Bible EVERY DAY. The best place to get to know who Christ is, what His miraculous works were and what His personal suggestions are on how to live out a "Christ – like" life is in the first four books of the New Testament {Matthew, Mark, Luke and John} Those books will take you from the Miracle of His Birth to the Celebration of His Death, Resurrection and Ascension.

 *Build and sustain a daily habit of meaningful and fervent prayer. Set aside some private time EVERY DAY to fellowship with God. Stop and examine in truth how much time you normally spend praying every day. Let's just say for the sake of example that you pray at least once a day for about 15 min. {Sadly, for some of us that would be stretching it} But, let's say that 15 min. is about right. Go ahead and make a covenant agreement with God today that you are going to increase your prayer life by 5 minutes per day each week until you get to an hour a day of fervent prayer. That's 20 minutes next week – 25 minutes the week after that – 30 minutes a week after that and so on until you get to hour. I guarantee you that when you get past the 30 minute point, things will start happening to you that will blow your mind. You may find yourself weeping or laughing or praying in a prayer language. You may even discover at that point that when you run out of things to say to God – God may have a few things to say you.

*Build and sustain a habit of regular worship in a Bible believing, Holy Ghost filled, Hand raising, Bible thumping Worship Center where the Word is taught fearlessly without political correctness.

 *And make absolutely sure that you hang out with people in your circle of friends that love God as much or more than you do.

Step 4.Meeting Him… When you have heard about somebody that sounds interesting enough that you want to find out more about them, then more than likely you will seek them out. When there is that much interest and you have gone to that much trouble to try to get to know them, it's a really great moment when you finally meet them. I have always given credit to my son for actually leading me to Christ but I know now that it was Christ {not my son Asa} who arranged the meeting.

I say that now because I know Christ said in John 15:16:

"You did not choose me, but I chose you and appointed you so that you might go and bear fruit – fruit that will last – and so that whatever you ask in my name the Father will give you."

Step 5.Accepting Him… Actually accepting Christ was an experience that literally brought me to my knees because of the desperate place I was in when I finally actually met Him.

I was in my 2 Corinthians 7:10 moment:

"Godly sorrow brings repentance that leads to salvation and leaves no regret, but worldly sorrow brings death. See what Godly sorrow has produced in you: what earnestness, what eagerness to clear yourselves, what indignation, what alarm what longing what concern, what readiness to see justice done."

That night at the end of my rope I found hope when I confessed with my mouth that Jesus is Lord and believed in my heart that God raised him from the dead. But folks - this is <u>not</u> where the work of salvation ends. NOW COMES---

Step 6.Getting to know Him…Come on people, we all know through life experience that we don't REALLY know somebody when you first meet them or accept them as a friend. It takes time being around that person to really "know" them. WHY? Because, you have to "experience" them. You need to find out what's going to be required of <u>YOU</u> to maintain the relationship. AND when you find out over time what Jesus requires to call you friend – it may be a deal breaker for you. { I hope not.}

111

How about this requirement in Mark 8: 34 – 38???

Then He called the crowd to him along with his disciples and said:

*"Whoever wants to be my disciple {friend} must deny himself and take up **his** cross and follow me. For whoever wants to save their life will lose it, but whoever loses their life for my sake and the gospel will save it. What good is it for someone to gain the whole world {material wealth and power} in exchange for their soul. If anyone is ashamed of me and my words in this adulterous and sinful generation, the Son of Man will be ashamed of them when He comes in his Father's glory with the holy angels."*

What about Christ's ideas about who is blessed.

"Blessed are the poor in spirit, blessed are those who mourn, blessed are the meek, blessed are those who hunger and thirst for righteousness, blessed are the merciful, blessed are the pure in heart, blessed are the peacemakers, blessed are those who are persecuted because of righteousness. And blessed are you when people insult you, persecute you and falsely say all kinds of evil things against you because of me. Rejoice and be glad..." {Matthew 5}

Being a friend of Christ and living in Him and for Him involves lots of "serving" and "suffering" and "sacrifice." But I have found that it is SOOO worth it.

Step 7. Trusting Him... In John 14:1 Christ asks us to do this:

"Do not let your hearts be troubled, trust in God, trust in me also."

The Word says that without faith you cannot please God. Hebrews 12 describes faith as being sure of what you hope for and certain of what you cannot see. If you are willing to trust Christ in faith – then through experience – you will begin to trust Him in deed as well.

Step 8. Obeying Him…God's Word reminds us that "obedience is greater than sacrifice." Learning to become obedient to the Sound Biblical Principles put forth in God's Word, rather than being a slave to the jacked up, ever-changing, dark and depraved principles of living found in the world today, will bring you a freedom and a joy in life that is beyond what you might imagine. Once you have gotten to the point in your relationship that you truly "know" and "trust" Christ Jesus – obedience comes easily. Believe me when I tell you that unconditionally submitting yourself to Christ as the complete authority over your life and constantly obeying His commands will bless you, your life and your family. Here are just a couple of God's promises concerning obedience.

Romans 2: 13 – *"For it is not those who hear the law who are righteous in God's sight, but it is those who <u>obey</u> the law will be declared righteous.*

1 John 2:5 - *"But if anyone <u>obeys</u> his Word, love for God is truly made complete in them. This is how we know we are in him."*

And this in Matthew 28:18 – 20: *"Then Jesus came to them and said, all authority in Heaven and on Earth has been* *given to me. Therefore, go and make disciples of all the nations, baptizing them in the name of the Father and of the Son and of the Holy Spirit, and teaching <u>them to obey</u> everything I have commanded <u>you</u>."*

Step 9. Submitting to him…Here it is in Hebrews 12:1-2:

"Therefore, I urge you brothers, in view of God's mercy, to offer your bodies as a living sacrifice, holy and pleasing to God – this is your spiritual act of worship. Do not conform any longer to the pattern of this world, but be transformed by the renewing of your mind. Then you will be able to test and approve what God's will is – his good, pleasing and perfect will."

Step10. Living <u>for</u> Him…Congratulations! You heard about Him. You found out about Him. You sought Him out. You finally met Him. Then by accepting Him you got to know Him. You finally got to the point that because you trusted Him you could now obey Him. So, in obedience you submitted to Him.

When you get this far into the Process of Salvation you will clearly know – "It's too late to turn back now." So begin now to live for Him in the context of Hebrews 12:14-15 which challenges us to:

"Make every effort to live in peace with all men and be Holy.{separated out from the world} *Without Holiness no one will see the Lord."*

So now we have reached the final step we can take in the Salvation Process while we are still on this earth and that step is:

Step 11.Living in Him…2 Corinthians 5:17 is what I often refer to as the "litmus test" for determining whether or not we are truly living "in Christ." It says:

"If a man be in Christ, he is a new creation, the old is gone and the new is come."

SOOO, I can stand up in front of the mirror, look into it and let God ask me in truth – "What's 'NEW' about you, Charlie Haynes?" "Well let's see. I don't have to throw a string of profanity into everything I say to make my point anymore. I don't lay my head down on my pillow drunk every night like I did for twenty years of my life. I don't have to wait till everybody in the house is asleep to go watch porn on the internet. And, I don't have to worry about what lie I am going to tell my wife about where I was and who I was with last night. Wow, I'm starting to feel good about the 'NEW' me already." Uh, Oh! Now God is wanting me to look back in that mirror one more time so he can ask me a MUCH more important question in truth.

"Ok, Charlie Haynes that all sounds good but let me ask you about the second part of the "litmus test" – What's 'OLD' about you?" There you are. The proof that you and I are "living in Him" is not determined only by what you have been willing to "let go of" but in God's eyes it is also determined by what you are "still holding on to" from your past life. Go to the mirror often my friend and question yourself in TRUTH until you are absolutely sure the "NEW" has come and the "OLD" is completely gone.

1 Corinthians 1:4 –9: *"I always thank my God for you because of his grace given you in Christ Jesus. For in him*

you have been enriched in every way – with all kinds of speech and with all knowledge – God thus confirming our testimony about Christ among you. Therefore, you do not lack any spiritual gift as you eagerly wait for our Lord Jesus Christ to be revealed. He will also keep you firm to the end, so that you will be blameless on the day of our Lord Jesus Christ. God is faithful who has called you <u>into fellowship with his Son</u>, Jesus Christ our Lord."

Now comes the final and everlasting step in the Salvation Process – the step that God sent his Son for – the step Christ died on the Cross for – and the step every man and woman on this earth should live to attain:

Step12. Reigning with Him for eternity in the Kingdom of Heaven!!!

Here is the final request of Christ to His Father in prayer {concerning us} just before going to the Cross of Calvary – John 17:24:

"Father, I want those you have given me to be with me where I am, and to see my glory, the glory you have given me because you loved me before the creation of the world.

Life Lesson Number Sixteen

16. God is not bound by my circumstances.

When men and women come to us at Righteous Oaks Recovery Center for Men or Jacob's Well Recovery Center for Women - whether of their own volition or sent into our programs by agencies like DHS or Drug Court or Parole Probation or by local churches, they come almost always in a condition of hopelessness and despair because of the place they have found themselves in life. By the time we see them, they have hit "rock bottom." They have lost their marriages, their children, their jobs, their homes, their families, their decency, and their freedom. I have been there in my own life. I too placed myself in a situation, due to the poor choices I was making in life, to lose everything and carry that burden of absolute hopelessness. I thank God that there are MANY people who will never have to experience those consequences but I lament that those same people find it hard to accept the fact that that - that friend or family member that has gotten caught up in the drug culture can't just straighten up, stop using and get their life back together. Sadly, those who have not gotten caught up in that life don't fully understand what it means when you say "so-in-so is a drug addict." Being a drug addict goes WAY deeper than just using drugs. It is an ever spiraling downward life for men and women that will carry them into the depths of depravity - just to survive. My experience has been that it is even worse for women because they can be "used" by those driving the culture as pawns in a dangerous and deadly game. A woman who is a drug user on the street is subject to being constantly disrespected, injected, beaten, molested, raped, pimped out, enslaved and whatever else she can be used for at the hands of those that simply consider her a piece of meat.

When a family member or friend comes up to me {often} and says, "Pastor Charlie, I don't know how you and your family can do this. Our family finally just had to throw our hands up and tell our child to get out – because we just couldn't take it anymore. We were just dealing with the one so I know it must be really hard on you guys to be dealing with thirty – five or forty at one time like y'all do here."

I always just give them a warm smile and say: "No Ma'am {or Sir} it's not a problem for us at all. The difference between your circumstances and ours is that, because you are family – you are 'emotionally involved in the problem' but we are 'Spiritually involved in the solution'."

And we know something through almost twenty years of doing this. That those people who come into our programs, don't come with a "problem with drugs" – they have a problem with "what has gone on in their hearts" that makes them turn to drugs and bad relationships. And we further know through our own life experience as a family that there is someone who can heal that broken heart and place ANYONE back into their true destiny – His name is Jesus Christ.

I have tried to seek the wisdom to help concerned family members and friends understand why: "They they just can't QUIT living that life." And here is how I try to explain it.

Let's just say that I sat you down in a straight back wooden chair. Then I took about a fifty foot long nylon rope and tied you to that chair as tightly as I possibly could from the end of your nose to the tip of your toes. And then, I backed up a few feet and shouted to you as loud a I could – "GET UP!!!" Would you be able to get up? NO! If a shouted – "LIFT YOUR HANDS IN PRAISE!!!" Could you do it? NOPE! If I urged you – "GET DOWN ON YOUR KNEES AND PRAY!!!" Would that be possible? I doubt it. What if I finally declared – "WHY DON'T YOU JUST GET UP AND WALK AWAY FROM THIS SITUATION?" Could you? NO WAY! And, why is that you ask?

BECAUSE YOU ARE <u>BOUND</u>!!!

And when you are bound that tightly and that completely whether it is physically, emotionally or spiritually you <u>CAN NOT</u> unbind yourself. It takes someone outside of the circumstances you have found yourself in to loose you. In the case of those of us who have found ourselves bound up as a consequence of what we have been through in life, I strongly believe that only God can effectively loose those bonds through the saving and transformational power of Christ.

2 Peter 2:19 reminds us:

"They promised them freedom, while they themselves are slaves of depravity – for people are slaves to whatever has mastered them."

Broken Hearts, Broken Promises and Broken Dreams can BIND you.

Lamentations 1:14 says:

"My sins have been "BOUND" into a yoke,
By God's hands they were woven together.
They have been hung on my neck,
and the Lord has sapped my strength.
He has given me into the hands
of those I cannot withstand."

I want to remind you that we have been warned in Romans 11:32 that God will allow those who choose to serve the world over serving God suffer the full consequences of those choices when He says:

"I will turn all men over to disobedience so that I may
have mercy on them."

According to what I have observed over all these years in my life and the lives of the thousands of men and women and their families we have ministered to: The GOOD NEWS is that when we turn back to Him – Mercy WILL come running!

Here is why I confidently say that – Job 36:5-12:

"God is mighty, but he despises no one;
he is mighty, and firm in his purpose.
He does not keep the wicked alive
but gives the afflicted their rights.
He does not take his eyes off the righteous;
he enthrones them with Kings
and exalts them forever.
But if people are bound in chains,
,held fast by the cords of affliction,

he tells them what they have done-
that they have sinned arrogantly.
He makes them listen to correction
and commands them to repent of their evil.
If they obey and serve him,
they will spend the rest of their days in prosperity
and their years in contentment.
But if they do not listen,
they will perish by the sword
and die without knowledge
{ Be advised and be forewarned. God has spoken!}

Life Lesson Number Seventeen

17. People do what they do because they believe what they believe.

It is a cold hard fact of life that people do what they do because they believe what they believe. Proverbs 23:7 puts it this way:

"As a man thinks in his heart, so is he."

Have you ever just stopped and examined yourself "in truth" as to what beliefs drive your life?

"A man who does not know where he is going will take any path to get there."

"A man who does not stand for something will fall for anything."

"Thinking you are on the right track means nothing if you're moving in the wrong direction."

I spent most of the first 50 years of my life living as a selfish, arrogant, ignorant, depraved, perverted, lying, manipulating, dishonest, faithless man because I "believed what I believed."

I believed that a relationship with God {if there was one} would "rain on my parade" concerning the way I intended to live my life.

I believed I was smart enough to get through this life successfully living by my own craftiness without any help from anybody on earth or <u>in Heaven</u>.

I believed if I ever did need advice on a problem, I could find someone else as devious as I was to partner up with me to help me get what I wanted.

I believed I was the "center of the universe".

I believed that the terrible consequences that I often found myself in you to the bad choices I was making were just a product of "bad luck."

I believed that there was no problem {no matter how big} that I could not run from.

I believed that the more people I could find to join me in the bad behaviors I practiced, the more okay it made the bad behavior. {You know, the old everybody is doing it excuse}

I was arrogant enough to believe that no matter how big of a mess I left behind in the wake of my selfish and destructive behavior toward others, I could always go back and clean it up.

I always believed I was too "slick" to get caught and believed the old saying: "What they don't know won't hurt 'em." But I finally learned "the hard way" the truth of God's Word as stated in Luke 12:2 –3:

"There is nothing concealed that will not be disclosed, or hidden that will not be made known. What you have said in

the dark will be heard in the daylight, and what you have whispered in the ear in the inner rooms will be proclaimed from the roof tops."

Finally, at 52 years of age {when I'm faced <u>MY</u> rock bottom moment} I began to realize that what I had believed all those years was a pack of lies and discovered the undeniable truth was – God always had a blueprint on the table that outlined my destiny and his plan and purpose for my life. And, in spite of my ignorance and unbelief, the plan was still on the table. As He does for all of us, He waited patiently through my years of disobedience for me to turn back to him – receive his mercy and forgiveness and step into the destiny the purpose for me before I was "knit in my mother's womb".

Although like many of you, even though it seems I had to learn every Life Lesson the Hard Way, today I am walking out that destiny and loving every minute of it.

The Reason…

Because today and for the rest of my life I have chosen to live by those beliefs that constantly bring: Love, Joy, Peace, Patience, Kindness, Goodness, Faithfulness, Gentleness and Self Control. And as God reminds us: "Against those things there is no law."

So, let me end this Chapter by sharing with you the <u>REAL TRUTHS</u> I have come to believe that now drive my life, my marriage, my relationships, my friendships and my Ministry.

*I believe that there is only one God and His name is **<u>Yahweh</u>**.

*I believe that He is the Creator of all things in Heaven and in Earth.

*I believe that He is the God of Abraham, Isaac and Jacob.

*I believe that He is the Lord and Father of my Savior Jesus Christ.

*I believe that He loved me so much that He sent his only begotten Son to this world to suffer and die on the Cross of Calvary so that {even though I had lived a sinful life} through my faith in Him I would not perish but have everlasting life.

*I believe that my Saviors name is **<u>Yeshua</u>**.

*I believe that He suffered on the Cross of Calvary for my sin and my sake.

*I believe He died there was buried and was subsequently raised from the dead.

*I believe that He ultimately ascended into Heaven where He sits even now at the right hand of the Father interceding for me against the "Accuser of this World."

*I believe that in His absence He has placed a deposit in me the Holy Spirit of God who will lead me, teach me, correct me, rebuke me and guide me through life on this Earth until I go to spend eternity with Him in Heaven.

*I believe as a Christian that I should believe and receive God's Word as given to us in the Old and New Testament writings from Genesis 1:1 to the end of Revelation and <u>APPLY THEM</u> to my life daily.

*I believe that the only way to be given the Assurance of Eternal Life through Salvation is to declare my sins, repent of them, confess with my mouth that Christ is Lord of my life {by that I mean He has complete authority over my life} and believe in my heart that He was truly raised from the dead.

*I believe that my Father in Heaven expects me to offer myself up to Him for the rest of my life as a living sacrifice, holy and pleasing to him; to turn my back the ways of the world and conform to them no longer; to allow my mind to be transformed and renewed by a constant washing in the Word so that I might discover His plan and purpose for my life and become a walking living testimony to His Mercy, Grace and Power.

*I believe I should determine to **BELIEVE** God and not just believe **<u>IN</u>** God.

*Therefore, I believe **<u>I AM</u>** who His Word says I am. **<u>I HAVE</u>** what His word says I have. And I **<u>CAN DO</u>** what His word says I can do.

<u>And that is</u> – "To make this final choice on what beliefs will drive the way I live the rest of my life."

Life Lesson Number Eighteen

18. Love is really a "Five Letter" Word

You and I and everyone must face the harsh and bitter reality that this world has watered down, diluted, polluted, twisted, tainted, misused, abused and perverted the "four letter word" <u>LOVE</u> to the point that it truly doesn't mean anything anymore. Today, we might say: "I love my mom or my wife or my children."

But, we might also say: "I love my dog." "I love my new car." "I love a cold Coke." "I love a hot pizza." "I love watching an X-rated video." "I love getting high." "I love getting drunk." "I love showing others whose boss" and on and on and on.

No wonder when we consider all the different misuses and misrepresentations of the word "LOVE" we are confused about what it really means and how to express it. How can that word have any credible meaning to someone who's being told that they are loved one minute and then being physically, mentally and emotionally abused by that same person in the next minute? – and yet we hear about those things happening all the time. How can that word have any meaning if it has to come with conditions and strings attached? You know, the old if you loved me you would... {Fill in the blank} You can call it manipulation, gratification, fascination, habitation, inclination, captivation, desperation or fornication. But what you have really got right there my friend is an <u>ABOMINATION</u> – not love. Not the "Five Letter" kind of love that we need to be looking for.

The good news is that since the beginning of creation, <u>God</u> has never been confused about what LOVE is supposed to mean and how it is to be demonstrated by those of us who LOVE Him.

Although the world's definition of the word LOVE is almost always presented in the context of feelings or emotions arising from the "needs of the flesh," "the lust of the eyes," and the "pride of life," God gives us a much more meaningful description of what <u>REAL LOVE</u> {"five letter love"} is and is not.

Only <u>ONE</u> word sufficiently and accurately describes the true definition of LOVE and that word used over and over throughout the Bible is the Greek word "AGAPE" – a selfless, sacrificial, compassionate, merciful, and forgiving LOVE – a LOVE that does not come from the emotions of God but rather by the Will of God and is a LOVE which defines God and is further demonstrated by Christ at the Cross of Calvary.

Here is what 1 John 4: 7 – says about God's love:

*"Dear friends, let us love one another, for love comes from God. Everyone who loves has been born of God and knows God. Whoever does not love does not know God, because "**God is love.**" This is how God showed us his love among us: He sent his one and only Son into the world that we might live through him. This is love: not that we loved God, but that he loved us and sent his Son as an atoning sacrifice for our sins. Dear friends, since God so loved us, we also ought to love one another. No one has ever seen God, but if we love one another, God lives in us and his love is made complete in us."*

Christ Jesus validated the power of AGAPE LOVE once and for all and forever when He came to this Earth in obedience to the Father to offer Himself as the perfect sacrifice for man's sins. In love, He established His ministry, left His legacy of His miraculous works coupled with His word, His will and His way chronicled in the New Testament writings of Matthew, Mark, Luke and John. He completed that work in love on the cross.

"When they had come to the place called the Skull, they crucified him there, along with the criminals – one on his right, the other on his left. And then Jesus said, Father, forgive them, for they know not what they do." {Luke 23:33-34}

It's important to understand that through that demonstration of AGAPE LOVE love He wasn't just dying for the righteous – on the contrary, He was dying for every sinner that would ever walk this Earth that they might later turn to Him as Savior and be given eternal life in the Kingdom of Heaven in spite of their past.

1 Timothy 1: 15 – 16 puts it this way:

"Here is a trustworthy saying that deserves full acceptance: Christ Jesus came into the world to save sinners – of time I am the worst. But for that very reason I was shown mercy so that in me, the worst of sinners, Christ might display his unlimited patience as an example for those who would believe on Him and receive eternal life."

And then, in John 15: 12 – 14 there is this:

"My command is this: love each other as I have loved you. Greater love has no one than this, that he would lay down his life for his friends."

The word is full of what I call "personal inventory Scriptures" the ones that I want to call to your attention today have to do with holding up the lies that we have been told and have begun to believe to the light of the truth of God's word. Stop and think for a moment about any important relationship that you have found yourself in whether it be family or friend or lover or spouse. Think about what you have accepted as proof of how much they love you and what you have settled for. Now let's go hold up that definition of love against God's definition of what love should be. You can find the "God's Love Check-off List" in1 Corinthians 13:4 –8. There you will find all 16 behaviors that must be in a relationship before God Almighty will call it love. I want you to go back and read them for yourself later, but here they are.

Love is patient {enduring, tolerant, forebearing}

Love is kind {considerate, goodhearted}

Love does not envy {resent}

Love does not boast {brag}

Love is not proud {arrogant, prideful}

Love is not rude {offensive}

Love is not self seeking {selfish}

Love is not easily angered {enraged}

Love keeps no record of wrongs {harbor un-forgiveness}

Love does not delight in evil {wicked behavior}

Love rejoices with the truth {as defined God's Word}

Love always protects {shields and defends}

Love always trusts {places confidence in}

Love always hopes {expects}

Love always perseveres {strives in spite of difficulties}

Love never fails {proves inadequate}

Stop settling and begin to insist that these 16 things are going to become the standard by which you measure the depth of someone else's love for you and the standard by which you measure your love for others. If you are not going to insist on those standards and are going to be satisfied living your life with whatever your relationships have to offer – good or bad – then I wish you well. But could you do this ONE THING for me and for my Father in Heaven – just PLEASE stop calling it LOVE.

Life Lesson Number Nineteen

19. The greatest gift you will ever give is the "Gift of Forgiveness"

Recently, I was looking at some statistics on the leading causes of death in the United States of America. I don't think it came as any surprise to me when I saw that Heart Disease, High Blood Pressure, Cancer, Stroke, Deep Depression and Suicide made it into the top causes. But there was <u>one cause</u> that really surprised me. As a matter of fact, this particular condition was given credit by several noted Doctors and Psychiatrist as the "ROOT CAUSE" of each of those afore mentioned conditions. And that "<u>root cause</u>" is a condition known as **UN-FORGIVENESS.** If you are like me, you are probably scratching your head and saying –**WHAAAT???**

When you get a minute go to your computer and Google in Health Warnings Concerning Un-Forgiveness and just watch what pops up. You might think it would be a bunch of sermons but no, it will be study after study of how dangerous the condition of un-forgiveness can be to your health and happiness in life if it is not dealt with. So for me, the search was on to discover why this destructive life condition could have so much power over us that it can <u>kill</u> us. I learned that, since the beginning of time, this condition has done more to destroy individual lives, families and friendships than any other condition known to man. It is a potent and destructive mixture of bitterness, hurt, anger, hostility, hatred, resentment, betrayal and fear constantly infecting the spirit, mind and body. This condition roots itself so deeply within us that there has been NO cure – no tablet, no elixir, no vaccination, no scientific concoction of any kind made by man that can cure it.   The most frightening aspect of this life destroying condition is that left unchecked it can actually cost you your soul. **BUT thank God, there is a cure!** Since you are into this book this far, it probably won't surprise you that now that I have heard what "MAN" says about it – I'm going to get in my Word and see what GOD says about it.

Let me start by saying that FORGIVENESS is a REALLY BIG DEAL to God. Why? Because God sent His only begotten Son into this world to be disrespected, abused, beaten, tortured and crucified so you and I could BE FORGIVEN.

"For God so loved the world that he gave his only begotten son, that whosoever believed in him should not perish, but have everlasting life. {John3:16}

AND THEN THIS:

As Jesus breathed His Last breath on the Cross of Calvary, He made this final request of His Father in Heaven: "Father, forgive them for they know not what they do." {Luke 23:34}

Yet in spite of following this awesome example of life's greatest gift; you and I would rather follow the example set forth by the unforgiving debtor talked about in Matthew 18:21 – 35 which begins by Jesus saying:

"Therefore, the Kingdom of Heaven is like a certain King who wanted to settle accounts with his servants. As he

began the settlement, a man who owed him 10,000 talents {millions of dollars} was brought to him. Since the man was not able to pay, the master ordered that he and his wife and his children and all that he had be sold to repay the debt.

{It was a tradition in those times that if a person ran up a debt they could not pay, the one owed the money could sell the debtor, his family and if necessary his fortunes to satisfy the debt}

But as the story goes <u>this</u> servant fell down on his knees and pled with the king for mercy and forgiveness saying:

"Be patient with me and I will pay back everything."

So the debtor is like: "Please, please, please King, just put me on an installment plan or something and I promise I'll pay back the money."

And guess what the King did? The Word says that the King "took pity on him" and basically said:
"Hey, you know what? Since you have humbled yourself and pled with me for mercy, tell you what I gonna do. Your debt is completely forgiven. You don't owe me diddly. Go in peace!" Now you would think that on the heals of that outcome, that the debtor would have walked away with a grateful and forgiving heart- <u>BUT-</u> Oh, No!!! That man when he walked outside met a man who owed <u>HIM</u> a hundred denarii {which is "chump change"} He grabs the poor fellow by the throat – starts choking him and yelling at him in front of all the onlookers saying:

"PAY ME WHAT YOU OWE ME!"

Then the fellow servant fell on <u>his</u> knees and began to plead:

"Please sir, be patient with me and I will pay you back."

What do you think He should have done based on how he was treated by the King just a few minutes before-Forgive the debt?

<u>Well, that's not what happened.</u>

The unforgiving/unmerciful servant refused and had the man thrown into prison till he could pay the debt. And here is where you and I can learn how God feels about "forgiven people" who refuse to "forgive others."

Matthew 18:31 – 35:
"When the other servants saw what had happened, they were greatly distressed and went and told the King everything that had happened outside. Then the King called the "unforgiving debtor" back in and said: "You wicked debtor, I canceled all that debt of yours because you begged me to.

Ok, hang on folks and understand what God is saying in this next verse.

"Shouldn't you have had mercy on your fellow servant just as I had on you?"   In anger the King turned the unforgiving debtor over to the jailers to be tortured until he paid back all he owed." And then Jesus said, "This is how my Heavenly Father will treat each of you unless you forgive your brother from your heart."

135

There is no human being walking this planet that has not done something in your life that you have regrets about – wish you could go back and change – and want to be forgiven for. Christ is the personification of forgiveness. You cannot truthfully say that you are Christ-like or "in Christ" if you are not ready and willing to forgive others who have hurt you - their mistakes in life. What we refer to as "The Lord's Prayer" ends with this powerful warning:

"For if you forgive men when they sin against you, your Heavenly Father will also forgive you. But if you do not forgive men their sins, your Heavenly Father will not forgive your sins."

When you and I are praying that same "Lord's Prayer" we say this at one point:

*"Forgive us our debts {sins/trespasses} **AS WE** have also forgiven our debtors {those who have sinned against us or trespassed on us}.*

Stop and think about how you forgive others each and every day and then ask yourself in truth. Do I REALLY want God to forgive me today the same way I'm forgiving everybody else? MAYBE NOT!

Ephesians 4:32 says:

"and be ye kind one to another, tenderhearted, forgiving one another, even as God FOR CHRIST'S SAKE hath forgiven you."

Knowing God, Believing God, Trusting God and coming to understand His deep concern for your joy and success in life makes His willingness to forgive us for Christ's sake extremely valuable. There is no forgiveness in all of creation that is more important than the "forgiveness of God" and no one in all of creation takes the subject of forgiveness more seriously than God. Therefore before we start worrying about the forgiveness we need to give people or that we want other people to give us, let's take care of the part about receiving God's forgiveness concerning what we've done to disappoint Him first.

Reminder: 2Corinthians 7:10 says:

"Godly sorrow brings repentance that leads to salvation and leaves no regret, but worldly sorrow brings death."

There is no more beautiful picture of how to approach God in deep need of forgiveness than in the picture painted in Luke 7:36-50 concerning the story of the "Sinful Woman."

As the story goes, Jesus was invited to a local Pharisee's house to have dinner. I think it's important to note that Christ knew {in spite of appearances} that He was not really an "Honored Guest" there since the Pharisees in general didn't have a very high opinion of Him. They mainly invited Him there, just to "check Him out." But Christ went anyway and reclined at the dinner table with the other guests.

Then Luke 7 tells us starting in Verse 37 that:

"When a woman who had lived a sinful life in that town{likely as a prostitute} learned that Jesus was eating at the Pharisee's house, she brought an alabaster jar of perfume, and as she stood behind him at his feet weeping,

*she began to wet his feet with her tears. Then she wiped
them with her hair, kissed them and poured perfume on
them. And when the Pharisee who had invited Jesus saw
this, he said to <u>himself</u>, "If this man were a prophet, he
would know who is touching him and what kind of a
woman she is – that she is a <u>SINNER</u>."*

There it is! The perfect picture of how we come to Christ
seeking forgiveness.

So, <u>Number One</u> - she had already heard, already knew
and already believed in Faith that if she could get to the
feet of Christ {no matter what the cost} she would be at
the feet of "forgiveness personified" and would no doubt
be forgiven there.

<u>Number Two</u>, she laid aside her pride and busted up inside
a place where she was neither invited nor welcome.

**Note: When you are coming to God for forgiveness,
there will be no room at the altar for your pride.**

Everybody in that room knew her reputation in that town –
what she was, where she had been, what she had done and
who she had been with. There of course was an excellent
chance that even some of those "religious men" in that
room might have spent a little time with her and were
sweating bullets when she showed up in the midst of them.

However, <u>Number Three</u> , she was NOT going to let the
judgemental attitudes of others or the shame of her own
past stop her from getting to the feet of forgiveness. They
say that the church rejoices when a new covert comes to

138

the altar but it sneers and passes judgement on a "back slider" who comes to repent. That's a shame.

But <u>don't you ever</u> let the shame of your past stand in the way of the forgiveness that awaits you ALWAYS at the feet of Christ.

And then as the story continues, another picture is painted of complete surrender and brokenness and humbleness at the feet of Christ. Normally it was the custom that the host of the dinner would have met Christ as an honored guest at the door when He first came in and do three things – wash His feet of the dirt and dust collected from walking the dirt paths where both men and livestock trod – give Him a kiss of greeting and anoint Him with "the oil of greeting"- none of which the host did for Jesus. But this sinful woman –

<u>Number Four</u> - broken, hurting and weeping fell at His feet. I can see now as the first of those profuse tears of joy poured down her face and fell on the dirty, dusty unwashed feet of Christ and how the moisture of each tear began to cleanse His feet one drop at a time. And in the depths of her humility and love for Him she took the hair of her own head and with those tears wiped the dirt and dust and dung from His feet - then kissed them and anointed them with the perfume she had brought.

That my friend is what sincere humility and brokenness looks like and the perfect picture of what mental, emotional and Spiritual condition we should be in we come to ask God for forgiveness.

And so now let's turn to the "Healing Power of Forgiveness" best demonstrated in my mind in Matthew 9:1-8.

Jesus stepped in to a boat, crossed over and came to his own town. Some men brought to him a paralytic, lying on the mat. When Jesus saw their faith he said to the paralytic, "Take heart, son; your sins are forgiven." At this, some of the teachers of the law said to themselves, "This fellow is blaspheming!" Knowing their thoughts, Jesus said, "Why do you entertain evil thoughts in your hearts?" Which is easier to say, "Your sins are forgiven," or to say, "Get up and walk?" But so that you may know that the Son of Man has authority on earth to forgive sins..." Then he said to the paralytic, "Get up, take your mat and go home." And the man got up and went home.

After witnessing this the paralytic's friend must have said to himself: Ok, hold on a minute! I've got this good friend who is paralyzed from the end of his nose to the tip of his toes. Now I've heard about this guy named Jesus and He is going all around the countryside day after day healing folks. He's healing the blind. He's healing the deaf. He's healing the crippled. He's healing the lepers.

He is casting out demons. Shoot – I've heard He's even raised the dead. Having heard that, me and a few of my buddies really <u>believed in faith</u> that if we could just get our friend in front of this Jesus – He could heal his paralysis. So, we load him up on a mat and we tote that sucker {a while}. We finally get him up in front of Jesus and He leans down over my buddy and says: "Take heart, son; your <u>SINS</u> are forgiven." Wait a minute! What does <u>that</u>

mean – "Your sins are forgiven?" We brought him here to get his paralysis healed – What is this "your sins are forgiven" stuff? Well, you see neither the paralyzed man nor his friends understood the underlying problem. What Christ knew that they did not know was that this man was paralyzed because of the un-forgiveness in his heart. The moment Christ said: "Take heart, son; your sins are forgiven – he was healed. He could have gotten up right then and walked away. But because he did not get the concept, Jesus had to say: "*so that you may know that the Son of Man has authority on earth to forgive sins..." Then he said to the paralytic, "Get up, take your mat and go home."*

Un-forgiveness will PARALYZE you.

I told you in an earlier chapter that at our Recovery Centers we are less concerned about the drugs that have been used and more concerned about the hearts that have been broken and the lies people tell themselves to be able to survive that heartbreak. Holding on to all the life altering – health destroying emotions that go with holding on to unforgiveness for a lifetime will result in a wasted life.

Webster's Dictionary tells us what "forgiveness" **is**: "Releasing someone from the consequences of an injurious act or crime" {Casting aside any further desire to "get even" or "pay back'}

BUT, It is also important for you to understand what it **is NOT.**

You are **not** saying, by forgiving someone, that what they have done to hurt you is OK. {in truth you are saying: What you did to be is an abomination and it hurt me deeply BUT, I am forgiving you so I don't have to spend the rest of my life bound by the bitterness it has caused me personally.}

There are four kinds of forgiveness – Three of them you control and one of them you do not.

The three kinds of forgiveness that you do control are:

1. The forgiveness of God. When you finally find yourself on your knees confessing the sin of your life {including the un-forgiveness you have harbored against those who have wronged you} – repeating of those sins and receiving Christ as Lord and Savior of your life – you will be immediately forgiven by Almighty God.

2. Forgiving yourself. Once you have received the forgiveness of God you must immediately begin the painful process of forgiving yourself for every misstep, mistake, misdeed, misbehavior, misconduct, misadventure and misguided decision. To not forgive yourself after you have received the most important forgiveness in all of creation {made possible by Christ's death} would be like you saying: "You know what God; the suffering and sacrifice that you allowed Your Son to go through just wasn't sufficient to cover MY SIN.

3. Forgiving others. So, I will just repeat what's already been said: "If we will forgive men their trespasses, our heavenly father will also forgive us: But if we forgive not men their trespasses, neither will our Father in Heaven forgive us our trespasses

And the one forgiveness <u>you do not control</u> is:

1. The forgiveness of others concerning what you have done to hurt them. You can't make someone else <u>forgive you</u> for the pain <u>you may have caused them.</u> Do <u>NOT</u> wallow in the self pity of not hearing someone forgive you for hurting them. Rather take the <u>guilt you are feeling</u> and <u>your desire to be forgiven by that person</u> and lay those two things {in prayer} at the foot of the Cross. My personal experience coupled with what I have observed God do in these situations over the last twenty years is that He {when He is ready} will eventually heal those relationships lost in your life if <u>He thinks</u> they are important enough.

I want to leave you all with one thing that God has placed in my spirit, and that is, that **un-forgiveness never dies**. It can be temporarily pushed aside. It can be numbed with alcohol and drugs. It can be forgotten in a moment of forbidden love. It can even be buried deep inside <u>but</u> it will be **buried alive**. As long as you allow un-forgiveness to remain in your life it will eventually **be ignored no longer**. It will eventually **sober up**. It will eventually **betray you**. It will eventually reach out its destructive hand from its burial place and pull you back into darkness and despair.

Un-forgiveness can only be defeated if it is laid at the foot of the Cross.

Today is the day to lay it down. Today is the day to give Christ Jesus, to give yourself and to give to those who's sins you hold against them the greatest gift you will ever give – **THE GIFT of FORGIVENESS.**

Life Lesson Number Twenty

20. If I Want To Stay Free – I Got To Stay Where I Got Free At!

I want to end this book by referring to a song - A song that Reverend Martin Luther King referenced at the end of his stirring speech on August 28th, 1963 given to millions on the Washington Mall and all around this world by radio and television. He referred to the song as: "that old negro Gospel Song" – Free at last, free at last, Thank God! I'm free at last!" I believe that in that moment birthed out of despair and heartbreak for a nation he truly loved – that was racked with bitterness and hatred – He was truly FREE – Free in Christ – as he was comforted by the words of that old Gospel Song imbedded in his heart!

Free at last, free at last
I thank God I'm free at last
Free at last, free at last
I thank God I'm free at last

Way down yonder in the graveyard walk,
I thank God I'm free at last
Me and my Jesus going to meet and talk
I thank God I am free at last

On my knees when the light passed by,
I thank God I'm free at last
Thought my soul would rise and fly
I thank God I'm free at last

Some of these mornings, bright and fair
I thank God I'm free at last

Going to meet King Jesus in the air
I thank God I'm free at last

Free because <u>HE</u> knew that the solution to the problems he was addressing so eloquently were at that moment and for all future moments in the Hands of God.

As we turn on our televisions or our radio or our computers or pick up a newspaper, we can be bound physically, emotionally and spiritually by the heart - breaking decline of not only our own society but the world as well. I have found great comfort in a couple of very important truths that I have learned from reading and studying God's Word, but more importantly, by choosing to <u>believe</u> what He says to me personally <u>in</u> his Word. Here are just a few of the comforting things He has taught me:

<u>"If I want to stay free – I am going to have to stay where I got free at!"</u>

***In His Word every single day – reading it, studying it and allowing Him to reveal His will for my life through it.

***On my knees every single day in private, personal, intimate time with Him – exalting Him, thanking Him, petitioning Him and listening to Him.

***Worshiping Him regularly in a church that fits the definition of that "Fellowship of Believers" described in Acts 2:42-47:

"They devoted themselves to the apostles teaching and to the fellowship, to the breaking of bread and to prayer.

Everyone was filled with awe, and many wonders and miraculous signs were done by the apostles. All the believers were together and had everything in common. Selling their possessions and goods, they gave to anyone as he had need. Every day they continued to meet together in the temple courts. They broke bread in their homes and ate together with glad and sincere hearts, praising God and enjoying the favor of all the people. And the Lord added to their number daily those who were being saved."

The kind of church once recommended by the great Bible Scholar - Dr. E.W. Bullinger:

"You ask, 'Where are you to worship?' We reply, 'Where ever God is glorified, Christ is exalted, God's Word is honored, the Holy Spirit's power is evidenced and 'man' abased.' Never go anywhere where you do not know more of God's Word when you leave than when you entered. Never be in any church body where you may be 'turned out', or have your name down where it may be scratched out.

Be content with the membership which God has given you in the spiritual unity of the Body of Christ, from which no power in Earth or Hell can cut you off and be content that your name was written in the Lambs "Book of Life" before the foundation of the world, and from which no power in Earth or Hell can ever take it out. Do nothing to imply that you do not hold these priceless privileges to be of infinite value; or that they can be added to in the slightest degree by any of man's corporate unities."

***It is for freedom that Christ has set me free. Therefore, I should stand firm then, and not let myself be burdened again by a yoke of slavery. Knowing that a man becomes a slave to whatever he allows to "master him."

***In faith, I can now walk out my destiny without fear of failure because God has convinced me that the Spirit of the Sovereign Lord is on me, because the Lord has anointed me to proclaim good news to the poor. Through the ministries that he has blessed me with, I know in my heart that he has sent me to "bind up the brokenhearted."

***I am further convinced that "this world" is not my home. Rather, I have been placed here by my Father in Heaven to do the work he called me to this Earth to do. And, when I have completed that work, He will take me out of "this world" to spend eternity with Him in heaven.

***I have come to the place where I know one thing for sure - that one day I will face death. On the other hand the two things that I do not know are how it will happen and when. That doesn't matter to me anymore because I have positioned myself where I am ready when He is.

I am also thankful for the fact that I have finally learned that "life" is not for saving. On the contrary, it is for giving away! 1 Corinthians 9:19 strengthens that belief in me when it says:

"Though I am free and belong to no one, I have made myself a slave to everyone, to win as many as possible."
{for Christ Jesus}

James 1:2 – 4 makes a statement that will make a worldly man or woman scratch their head in wonderment when it says:

"Consider it pure joy, my brothers, whenever you face trials of many kinds, because you know that the testing of your faith develops perseverance. Perseverance must finish its work so that you may be mature and complete, not lacking anything."

Ever heard the old saying, "no pain no gain"? Guess what? That is a biblical principle. God's word tells us that He cannot be tempted, nor does He tempt anyone. But rather we will be tempted when we are drawn away by our own evil desires. So, God <u>will</u> allow us to be tempted. Sometimes, as in my case, it seems we have to learn everything the hard way instead of God's way. What God has shown me is that once we <u>do</u> learn our lesson, He is quick to forgive. And He has also shown me time and time again, not only in my own life but in others - that on the other side of every trial, test and tribulation that we press through to gain the truth in Christ – there will be a blessing.

Being called to conduct a recovery ministry for men and women who are coming out of prison and off the street having been caught up in every dark, depraved and dangerous situation that the Gates of Hell could throw against them; invites the constant attack of Satan on the lives of those who serve here as well as the residents. Nevertheless we will rise every morning {as long as there is breath in our body} and strap on the belt of truth, the breastplate of righteousness, the shield of faith, the helmet of salvation and the sword of the Spirit, our feet fitted with the readiness of the gospel to march to the front lines to fight the "good fight." We will do that day after day, strengthening ourselves with the promise made in James 1: 25 which says:

"But who ever looks intently into the perfect law{of God} that gives freedom, and continues in it – not forgetting what they have heard, but doing it – they will be blessed in what they do.

And finally, on a personal note, thank you from the bottom of my heart for taking the time to read this book. If you know someone else that is struggling in life that you think it might help in some way, please tell them about it.

Each time you go to God in prayer, I would deeply and sincerely appreciate it if you would pray God's continuous protection and blessing over my wife, Pam, and I as well as the staff of our ministries and those who are resident in them.

Here is my heartfelt prayer for you and your family:

If you are going to stand,
stand for what you know is right.
If you are going to sit,
sit at the foot of the cross.
If you are going to walk,
walk the "straight and narrow path."
If you are going to speak,
speak the truth of God's Word.
If you are going to give,
give hope to the hopeless.
If you are going to take,
take on the burden of your brothers.
If you're going to live,

live for Christ.
If you are going to die, I pray you hear:
"Well done good and faithful servant."

THE END